DEAD BOYS CAN'T DANCE

Dead Boys Can't Dance

Sexual Orientation, Masculinity, and Suicide

MICHEL DORAIS
WITH SIMON L. LAJEUNESSE

TRANSLATED BY
PIERRE TREMBLAY

McGill-Queen's University Press
Montreal & Kingston · London · Ithaca

© McGill-Queen's University Press 2004
ISBN 0-7735-2653-6 (cloth)
ISBN 0-7735-2654-4 (paper)

Legal deposit second quarter 2004
Bibliothèque nationale du Québec

Printed in Canada on acid-free paper that is 100% ancient forest free
(100% post-consumer recycled), processed chlorine free.

McGill-Queen's University Press acknowledges the support of the Canada
Council for the Arts for our publishing program. We also acknowledge the
financial support of the Government of Canada through the Book Publishing
Industry Development Program (BPIDP) for our publishing activities.

Originally published as *Mort ou fif: La face cachée du suicide chez les garçons*,
VLB éditeur, 2001.

National Library of Canada Cataloguing in Publication

Dorais, Michel, 1954–
  Dead boys can't dance: sexual orientation, masculinity, and suicide /
  Michel Dorais with Simon L. Lajeunesse; translated by Pierre
  Tremblay.

  Includes bibliographical references.
  ISBN 0-7735-2653-6 (bnd)
  ISBN 0-7735-2654-4 (pbk)

  1. Gay youth – Suicidal behaviour – Quebec (Province). 2. Suicide –
  Prevention. 3. Homosexuality – Psychological aspects. I. Lajeunesse,
  Simon Louis, 1962– II. Title.
  HV6545.4.D6713 2004   362.282′086′64209714   C2003-905092-0

This book was typeset by Dynagram Inc. in 11/14 Garamond.

Contents

Introduction   3

1   What This Book Is About   8

2   Social Factors and Suicide   15

3   The Young Men Studied   27

4   Two Profiles, Four Scenarios   33

5   Life Situations   50

6   Isolation, Shame, and Stigmatization   74

7   Resiliency Factors   83

8   Recommendations for Suicide Prevention   90

9   Challenging Homophobia   106

Bibliography   115

Index   121

DEAD BOYS CAN'T DANCE

Introduction

Nicholas had for years been the target for hurtful homophobic comments by classmates without anyone at school ever intervening. As a model student, he never complained about the situation. Other boys did not consider him masculine enough, and the talk was that he was "a fag." One day as his class was passing the school's swimming pool, some boys threw him in, fully clothed. Everyone including the teacher had a good laugh. Nicholas was humiliated and distressed, and the event became the final straw. The next day he killed himself by jumping from the top of the village's railway bridge.

After his funeral, a recently hired teacher tried to sensitize the school to the possible relationship between the ostracism inflicted on Nicholas and his suicide. The man's efforts were met with the firm recommendation that he be silent on the issue, and his teaching contract was not renewed.

This story was told to us by Nicholas's mother a little less than a year after her son died. He was fifteen years old.

Jean-Philippe was an inquisitive adolescent involved with others and a confidant for many of his friends. In so many ways he was the kid that parents dream about having. However, he was deeply troubled by a great secret. After his sister found him hanging from a wooden beam in the family home, the note written just before his final act was discovered:

To all who love me and to the ones who did not love me. I am sick of this shit of a life. Sick, to the point of wanting to puke!!! I am so lonely. So alone with what I am suffering. I'd rather die than go on suffering like this.

Jean-Philippe xxx

PS: By the way, I was gay and I would like to say to the ones who still love me that I will never forget them.

In their attempts to retrace what could have happened to precipitate Jean-Philippe's crisis, his parents discovered that he had recently visited many Internet sites with homosexual content. Without doubt the revelation or the confirmation of his attraction to same-sex individuals caused him great distress, leading him to anticipate the worst. This is what his parents believe, but they insist they would have been supportive if their son had told them of his problems. Unfortunately we will never know exactly what Jean-Philippe was feeling, just as he will never know that his parents would have been much more accepting of his nature than he believed. He was fourteen years old when he died. It happened on a Saturday, the first time that Jean-Philippe ever failed to deliver the morning newspapers.

Not all youths who recognize their homosexual orientation contemplate or commit suicide, but this very important problem is often underestimated. In spite of accumulating studies with convincing evidence, there is ongoing reluctance to recognize the link between the traditional social stigmatization of homosexuality and the elevated incidence of suicide attempts and suicides by adolescent and young adult males identified as gay by themselves or by others. Further, the double taboo surrounding the problem means that homosexuality will generally not be talked about in the presence of young people, except negatively, and that the issue of youth suicide will also not be discussed.

As victims of heterosexism and homophobia, young homosexual individuals often feel overwhelmingly guilty for being who they are. If they are also thinking of ending their lives, they know they will be failing doubly in meeting the expectations of those closest to them, especially their parents. Parents in turn may feel doubly shamed: for having a homosexual son, and for having a suicidal son. These young men are twice "not like everyone else," meaning "not normal" in the eyes of others. As a result, their families are usually silent for fear of also being stigmatized.

Great courage is needed to end this silence, and we are therefore deeply grateful to the mothers of Nicholas and Jean-Philippe (not their real names) for giving us permission to write their stories. The teacher at Nicolas's school who was a little too curious and sympathetic and so did not get his contract renewed highlights the imposed "silence" problem. Sexuality issues surrounding youth suicide have long remained hidden and secret. Society apparently chooses silence in an attempt to shield the deceased's friends and family from further grief. In consequence, our misunderstanding continues.

Most young homosexual men who attempt or commit suicide take their secret to their graves. This happened to the "perfect boy who did not have any reason to end his life" but who nonetheless attempted and, unfortunately managed to kill himself. And the relatives of these young men do not report their suffering, for reasons previously noted. Our laws, especially in Canada, attempt to make all citizens equal, whatever their sexual orientation. Still, many gay or bisexual adolescents and young adults continue to be deprived of relevant information and support or help, even when they are systematically degraded, ostracized, and sometimes physically harmed. They may also be totally ignored because their non-existence is assumed. The underlying message is that homosexual people do not – should not – exist.

North American campaigns against sexism and racism during the past decades have produced positive results for women and minority ethnic groups. For young homosexual people, however, little has changed. True, some groups have formed to help them, especially in larger cities and sometimes in surrounding regions, but young people must first know that these groups exist. Unfortunately, many schools do not supply such information, fearing accusations of proselytizing. Homosexuality remains a taboo subject, and related resources continue to be withheld. The media present few of the positive images needed to counter the caricatures so often encountered. The media norm includes "fag" jokes and a generalized view of homosexuality as either tragic or comic. Consequently, young gay and bisexual people continue to die because they are so alone, often feeling that their fate is shared by no one else. Some believe themselves to be monsters, while others have lost patience with being the victims of ignorance. Some will die because they foresee no end to being judged negatively, despised, and rejected. As I write these lines, all of Quebec is in mourning for the death by cancer of a great sports hero celebrated for his courage and combative spirit. Surely equal or more tenacity is needed for gay young boys to endure jeers, hatred, and physical abuse because of their being different. They are not becoming "real men" as dictated by contemporary beliefs. From an early age they have had to endure the little-known, highly destructive social cancer that undermines self-esteem, faith, and trust in others, and the desire to live. This cancer is intolerance. Intolerance kills.

1

What This Book Is About

TERMINOLOGY

It is important at the outset to define the concepts used in this study of suicide attempts by adolescent and young men identified as homosexual by themselves and/or by others. *Contexts* here refers to the life situations of suicidal individuals, and *motives* refers to the factor(s) inciting them to act. The term *suicide attempt* refers to the behaviours that individuals have used deliberately to end their lives.

The volunteer study sample consists of young men (of eighteen to thirty-five years of age) who attempted suicide one or more times between the ages of fourteen and twenty-five years inclusively. In all cases medical and/or psychiatric care was requested after one or more suicide attempts. When interviewed, the majority of these young men, twenty-four of the thirty-two subjects, had been self-identified and/or identified by others as homosexual when they made the attempt. The remaining eight young heterosexual subjects form a small comparative group.

As adolescents, many of the so-called homosexual males did not identify themselves as homosexual, gay, or bisexual, but they were nonetheless believed to be homosexual or feared being identified as such in their living environments. Making this distinction seemed to us to be of importance.

SOME STATISTICS ON THE INCIDENCE OF ATTEMPTING SUICIDE BY YOUNG GAY AND BISEXUAL MEN

Suicide is well ahead of road accidents as a cause of death among young people in Quebec, the province with the highest suicide rate in Canada. Among young men aged fifteen to twenty-four years, the suicide rate is about seven times the rate for same-age females (Gouvernement du Québec, Conseil permanent de la jeunesse 1995: 48). Young women are many times more at risk than males for attempting suicide (Gouvernement du Québec, Direction générale de la santé publique 1997: 10); however, the high incidences of attempted suicide are not associated with higher suicide rates for females. The opposite applies for males. A larger proportion of young men who attempt suicide completed their act. Some of the reasons for this are explored in our study.

To date, Quebec researchers have not investigated the possible link between suicidal behaviours and individuals having a homosexual or bisexual orientation. In English Canada and the United States, however, the statistics produced have been widely reported and noticed.

In an effort to avoid the debate related to some quantitative studies lacking representation as noted by Remafedi (1994), we do not review studies based on unrepresentative volunteer samples. A survey of twelve such studies of gay and bisexual male youth from the United States and Canada produced an average lifetime incidence of 31.3 per cent for attempting suicide (Bagley and Tremblay 1997a). The main studies we review are those produced from large, mostly random samples of homosexual and bisexual males that have comparative samples of heterosexual males matched on the basis of selected demographic variables.[*] As a rule these studies report that homosexually oriented adolescent and young adult males are six to sixteen times more at risk for attempting suicide, either during their lifetimes or over a specified period of time, than their heterosexual counterparts.

The first such study was carried out by Bell and Weinberg (1978) during the late 1960s and early '70s on a large group of predominantly white and black homosexual males living in the San Francisco Bay area. The study reported that 37 per cent of homosexual males had considered suicide at some point in their lives and that 18.4 per cent had attempted suicide. A comparative group of heterosexual males randomly sampled in the same area indicated that up to their average age at the time they were studied (thirty-six years), homosexual males had been about six times more at risk of having attempted suicide than heterosexual males (ibid.). Joseph Harry, in a further analysis of the Bell and Weinberg (1978) data, also noted this higher risk factor (Harry 1994), especially at a young age. Little known to the public is that the data revealed that up to the age of seventeen years the relative risk factor was *much* higher: homosexual males at this age were about sixteen times more at risk for attempting suicide than their heterosexual counterparts.

The Bagley and Tremblay (1997a) study, the only one of its kind available in Canada, was carried out on a stratified random sample of 750 young men in Calgary, Alberta. It reported

---

[*] We only reference studies with whole or sub-samples of young homosexual and bisexual men, not studies of young gay and lesbian individuals combined. This is related to the nature of this study, which is exclusively focused on males.

that homosexual and bisexual young men, 12.7 per cent of the sample,[**] accounted for 62.5 per cent of the suicide attempters. The authors also reported that among the young men aged eighteen to twenty-seven years (mean, 22.7 years), the homosexual and bisexual males had been almost fourteen times more at risk for a suicide attempt than their heterosexual counterparts. These results basically replicate the results to the age of twenty years in the Bell and Weinberg (1978) sample.

In 1998 an analysis was published of a Minnesota sample of 36,254 students in grades seven to twelve, their mean age being fifteen years. In spite of limited numbers declaring themselves to be gay or bisexual (202 students), the homosexual and bisexual male adolescents were reported to have been seven times (28 per cent vs. 4.2 per cent) more likely to have attempted suicide in their lifetimes than their heterosexual counterparts (Remafedi et al. 1998: 57–60). A similar study was done by Garofalo et al. (1999) on a randomly selected Massachusetts sample of 4,167 students in grades nine to twelve. The 3.8 per cent of self-identified gay and bisexual males had a suicide attempt rate (over a period of twelve months) of approximately 33 per cent, compared to 5 per cent for their heterosexual counterparts. The analysis of a subsample of more than three thousand males by Cochran and Mays (2000) produced data on young men seventeen to twenty-nine years of age who reported having had same-sex partners. About 31.3 per cent of the former

---

[**] This percentage estimate corresponds to results from studies in which issues of anonymity and confidentiality were seriously respected. Whenever either of these elements is lacking, the percentages of individuals who report having had same-gender sexual experiences will be lower. On this subject, see Kinsey et al. (1948), *Sexual Behavior in the Human Male;* Hite (1983), *The Hite Report on Male Sexuality;* Janus (1993), *The Janus Report on Sexual Behavior;* Laumann et al. (1994), *The Social Organization of Sexuality.*

group had attempted suicide, compared to an incidence of 3.3 per cent for the group of males reporting not having had same-sex partners.

It must be noted, however, that youth suicide studies have not been designed to explore the significance of homosexuality in suicide deaths. Further, death certificates and families have usually been silent about the sexual orientations of deceased youths, even if a gay or bisexual orientation was known or suspected. The available data on post-mortems have also generally failed to supply information on the possible real motives for these suicides. That is, most young victims of suicide take their secrets to their graves, and the causes for their suicides are, almost by default, attributed to assumed "mental disorders."

Many studies of homosexually oriented youth were done on small volunteer samples to explore their risks for suicide problems. Two Internet sites developed by Pierre Tremblay, an independent researcher associated with the universities of Calgary and Southampton, supply an extensive listing of these studies and their published and unpublished results.[***] Here, we focus on the results of two Quebec studies, while making reference to other North American study results.

The Omega Cohort is an ongoing study of Quebec men who are having sexual relationships with other men. A preliminary analysis of about six hundred respondents of this cohort has revealed that 36 per cent of them attempted suicide at some point in their lives, and that almost twice this percentage contemplated suicide at least once. Alarmingly, almost 15 per cent of these men had attempted suicide more than once, their average age at the time of their first attempt being twenty (Otis

***http: //www.sws.soton.ac.uk/gay-male-suicide and
   www.virtualcity.com/youthsuicide/

et al. 2000). Another study carried out by the Quebec gay magazine *RG* reported that 44 per cent of the 125 respondents had contemplated suicide and that 26 per cent had attempted to end their lives (Dorais and Berthiaume 1998: 10–11). These results replicate other similar North American studies done in the last twenty-five years. One of the first, by Jay and Young (1977), reported that 40 per cent of the male respondents to a questionnaire had either seriously contemplated or attempted suicide. The previously noted Bell and Weinberg (1978) study reported similar percentages, with 58 per cent of homosexual suicide attempters specifying that their homosexual orientation was implicated in their attempt. Remafedi et al. (1991) studied 137 young gay and bisexual males ranging in age from fourteen to twenty-one years. They reported that about a third of the suicide attempts had occurred during the year that these young men had been identified as gay or bisexual, and almost half of the suicide attempters had attempted suicide more than once. The researchers associated with the Omega Cohort also expressed the belief that a link exists, at least for some young men, between the revelation of their homosexual or bisexual orientation – coming out – and the period of high risk for attempting suicide.

The cited results may suggest that having a homosexual orientation is causal in suicidality, but the evidence from studies indicates otherwise. Instead, it appears that having a homosexual or bisexual orientation *in highly homophobic environments* adds to many of the reported risks associated with suicide behaviours. Therefore, exploring this aspect was a major objective of our study, as opposed to seeking to establish a link between homosexual orientation and suicidal behaviours. This link, in our opinion, has been well established by other researchers. We have to go further in the explanation of this covaluation.

To summarize, although the high risk for suicidal ideation and behaviours in young gay men has been increasingly recognized, little is known about the factors actually implicated in this vulnerability. Our study therefore explored this vulnerability, the focus being on the improved understanding of situations associated with the suicide attempts of young gay and bisexual men. Whatever the magnitude of suicide and attempted suicide problems for these youths, an improved understanding of the contexts and motives implicated in so many of these cases is work to be done. Additionally, such research has great importance because these young men form part of the population that is largely ignored, not understood, or misunderstood by most people – including many mainstream suicidologists.

2

Social Factors and Suicide

What could be more personal than suicide? We can easily imagine an individual, alone and depressed, who takes his own life in some secluded location. Although the psychological nature of this act is undeniable, we have placed our study in a broader sociological context. In fact, we postulate that it is possible that suicide can be better understood and prevented if the problem is primarily constructed as a social phenomenon. Even though suicide is by definition a personal act, the individual who attempts it or the one who completes the attempt does not act in isolation from the contexts and motives stemming from life experiences that are social and have a history that should not be ignored.

To clarify the objective of our study, we adopt the definitions of suicide and attempted suicide used by Émile Durkheim in his work on the subject, originally published in 1897. From his point of view, suicide is the word designating all forms of death directly or indirectly stemming from an act, whether it is positive or negative, carried out by the victim who is aware of the fatal outcome. The attempt is the same act, but it was stopped before the fatal outcome occurred (Durkheim 1952).

Durkheim sought to demonstrate that sociology was not simply philosophy or psychology in disguise. He believed that varied elevated rates of suicide could not be only the result of mental illness. If the postulated madness of individuals committing such an act did not explain suicide, there must therefore be another explanation. He concluded that the other explanation would be sociological in nature.

Durkheim discovered that suicide, in fact, is far from being an isolated act. Suicide rates are relatively stable, and variations exist only in association with major social changes characterized by high stress levels. One's group associations are also a factor, including one's age group. On the basis of statistical data, Durkheim defined two axes along which variations occur in response to social attributes. The vertical axis represents social regulation, from strict or rigid rules at the upper end to an absence of rules at the lower end. The horizontal axis represents social integration, from exclusion on one side to total integration on the other. This axis represents the level of an individual's integration in a particular society or social subgroup. Along the two axes, four types of suicides emerge (see figure).

At the upper end of the social regulation axis, when the rules are as strict and rigid as possible, individuals kill themselves because they are overwhelmed by the demands of their social group. According to Durkheim, these are fatalistic suicides. Individuals do not perceive any other option but suicide because they cannot live up to the apparently moral rules of their social group. At the lower end of this axis, individuals commit suicide because rules are not available to guide them, thus resulting in anomie-related suicides; the individual does not know what to expect from life or society.

On the horizontal axis, complete exclusion from their group causes some individuals to feel alone in the world, and this outcome is unbearable for them. At the other end of the axis,

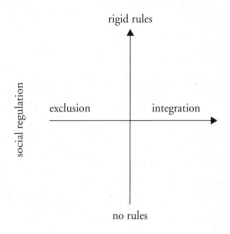

social integration

Axes of suicide according to Émile Durkheim

total fusion with a social group results in the loss of individuality. Such individuals kill themselves for the benefit of others, these being altruistic suicides. In this category are the suicides of the fanatically religious or political. For example, some individuals will use themselves to deliver a bomb so that the deemed enemies of their social group will be killed, like Kamikaze pilots in the Second World War and Palestinian suicide bombers today.

When a suicide occurs, the extremities of the above social regulation and integration axes are usually implicated. It should be noted that individuals located near the centre of the axes are the least inclined to commit suicide. In the following chapters, which describe interviews with young homosexual men who attempted suicide, the influence of two social-dimension attributes identified by Durkheim will become apparent. The expectations of social rules or demands that they could not adhere to were crushing these young men. They also experienced rejection, or felt they would be totally rejected, especially in their immediate environments, should they ever be recognized to be transgressors of social dictates.

In his book *Stigma*, Erving Goffman (1965) speaks of social integration and regulations in relation to stigma. He uses the term to refer to attributes that are deeply discrediting. But he emphasizes that the understanding of stigma is more related to perceiving it in social relationships. The creation of stigma is therefore the result of interactions between individuals, as opposed to being something particular carried by a person. Also, some discredited attributes may be without effect in certain environments, and they may also be valued, while in other environments they will not be accepted and will result in opprobrium.

In stigma situations, the individual may presume that his stigmatized attribute is evident and is therefore known to all, or the same stigmatized attribute may be disguised to avoid immediate detection. In the latter case, however, the danger lies in the fact that the stigmatized attribute is becoming a sword of Damocles. In the first case, the individual will be discredited, while in the second case the individual is discreditable, especially as a self-perception. Goffman places homosexuality mostly in the first category if the attribute is known or detectable. He also introduces the process of auto-oppression: it acts in response to internalized expectations and norms directed at the person by others. Individuals therefore do not need the presence of others to suffer from the discrepancy existing between who they are and what they should be. Even though the presence of the "normal ones" highlights and accentuates their "difference," stigmatized individuals can hate themselves in front of their own mirrors.

Faced with the impossibility of integration and with a lack of acceptance on the basis of their stigmatized attributes, individuals may respond in three ways. They may correct what is perceived to be an imperfection, as some males in our study did by attempting to become asexual or heterosexual. Secondly, they may work at mastering certain activities that the stigma would preclude as possible. Having adopted a disguise, they may seek perfection and be above reproach in these endeavours. The third possible response is situated in the rift between the individuals themselves and social conformity. In an ironic way, they will begin to act as is socially expected for individuals with the stigma. For example, some gay-identified males will begin to act out what is believed to be the stereotypical "fag." Given the belief that the stigma is somehow "contagious," socially acceptable people will avoid having close relationships with the stigmatized individuals, resulting in discrimination and social exclusion.

Howard Becker focuses on the culture of exclusion and of the social construction and organization of excluded people, those decreed for whatever reason to be "deviant." He also seeks to understand from a position within the culture of the excluded. Becker's beliefs, as embodied in *Outsiders* (1963), are an extension of those in Goffman's *Stigma*. Becker explores how stigmatized individuals live, think, and socially organize in their cultures.

Becker highlights the meaning of the word *outsider*. When a social rule is enforced, the person supposed to have broken it may be seen as a special kind of individual, one who cannot be trusted to live by the rules agreed on by the group. He is regarded as an outsider. The emphasis here is on the person "supposed to have broken" a social rule, because it often requires that an individual only be suspected of having transgressed a norm to be classed among the excluded. That is, the belief that someone has violated a social rule may be sufficient to establish that person's stigmatized status.

The norms make themselves known in two ways. They may be formally recognized through laws and their implementation, or they may be made known through less formal mechanisms such as tradition. In either case, certain individuals are entrusted with the task of having all norms in that society adhered to and respected. They may be specially dressed for the task, as is the case for police and many others who intervene in situations. The enforcers of norms include average individuals. Those deemed deviant with respect to a norm may either accept or deny that a transgression has occurred. They may also assert that the accusers are in error. In this way, they reject what is decreed to be socially "normal" and argue for what may become for the deviant individuals a behavioural norm.

Given that anyone suspected of a transgression of a norm could be labelled deviant, social deviance is therefore the result of a social interaction. Becker thinks of deviance as the product of a transaction that takes place between some social group and the one who is viewed by that group as a rule-breaker. He is therefore less concerned with the personal and social characteristics of deviants than with the process by which they come to be thought of as outsiders and with their reactions to that judgment. According to Becker, there are a number of ways for one to become deviant in a social setting, as summarized in the table on the following page (1963: 20).

Two of the situations need little explanation: the individual who obeys the norms and is perceived as such, and the "pure deviant" who does not deny his "marginality." The latter classification may apply, for example, to individuals believed to be homosexual and who in fact are. The other two cases are more complex. When the Kinsey study was published in 1948, we learned about the great extent to which secret deviance may exist, especially with respect to homosexuality. On the other

Table 1   Types of deviant behaviour according to Howard Becker

	Obedient behaviour	Rule-breaking behaviour
Perceived as deviant	falsely accused	pure deviant
Not perceived as deviant	conforming	secret deviant

hand, anyone can be accused of transgressing the heterosexual norm. There is no lack of historical cases where accusations of homosexuality (or sodomy) were used to oppress a group, as happened with the Templars and Cathars. What is believed to be real has very real consequences.

To better understand the dynamics of deviance, Becker uses the concept of *career*. All deviant careers are marked by a first act, deemed by the person or others to mark that person's entry into deviance. With respect to homosexuality, the judgment made in a young man's environment will therefore play an important role. The public revelation of his "deviance" is also a major turning point in his life. It is often at this moment that his identity changes in the eyes of other people, and the same may apply to his self-perception. He therefore acquires a new status – a process called "coming out." The last stage in a deviant career, according to Becker, consists of becoming a member of a group of others like oneself. The resulting feeling of allegiance and of belonging represents a significant step in the identity construction of the deviant, and the adhesion to a group deemed deviant by society produces two outcomes. There is a generally positive reconceptualization of the "deviant" status that may include highlighting the positive aspects of living on the margins. As well, these individuals will learn to live with a minimum of problems in spite of belonging to a group deemed to be deviant.

With respect to young gay men, becoming part of a group of similarly marginalized individuals who will help them overcome the prejudices and pressures to conform may be far from what actually happens. They are isolated, at least at the beginning, and at the mercy of those who assert that heterosexuality is the only normal outcome – meaning that it is compulsory. This pressure often takes the form of what Heinz Leymann calls "mobbing," a term synonymous with "moral harassment" (Hirigoyen 2000) or what others have called bullying: "By mobbing, we mean a form of communication that threatens the individual with great psychological and/or physical harm. Mobbing is a destructive process consisting of hostile behaviours which, when taken individually, could appear to be harmless, but their constant repetition produces very negative results" (Leymann 1996: 26–7).

Mobbing or moral harassment is therefore an interrelated group of behaviours consisting of statements, attitudes, and hostile responses directed at an individual and repeated over time. Moral harassment should not be confused with immediate and personality conflicts; we cannot get along with everyone all of the time. All situational or personality conflicts, however, do have the potential of becoming moral harassment if certain conditions apply.

The behaviours associated with moral harassment, if taken separately, may appear to be harmless. It is this interpretation that gives harassers such great power, possibly allowing them to act with impunity over long periods before the destructive process is recognized and confronted. Unfortunately, the burden of proof lies with the victim who has been discredited by the harassers, and the effects of the harassment on him and his living environment make the situation more difficult to correct. The same applies in affirming the rights of the harmed individual.

Leymann notes that mobbing victims must grapple with the prejudices and conflict of their abusers, and that certain groups are at greater risk for harassment than others. He therefore criticizes some psychologists for their failure to recognize the social interplay existing in harassment situations and for also placing all the blame on the victims. These problems are part of what homosexual people historically have had to endure. This includes being in work groups and classes organized with specific objectives most often only related to the social norms. So, the common assumption persists that everyone is heterosexual, or that homosexually oriented people form such small numbers that related issues can be ignored.

The work of David Plummer (1999) is of value here because it permits a better understanding of male youth suicide and its link to the stigmatization of homosexuality. Plummer's empirical study explores homosexuality and heterosexuality in relation to young men, as well as masculinity with its associated mythology. He shows that young men identified as homosexual generally experience both ostracism and moral harassment. For those not so identified but aware of their homosexual desires, being perceived as homosexual is a major fear because gay adolescents lack protection and respect. The study subjects often reported that their attempting suicide was related to their sexual orientation and related identification, to ostracism, and to the impossibility of believing that happiness and homosexuality were compatible.

As we have seen in the previous chapter, the risk for suicidal ideation and suicidal behaviours is significantly higher for young homosexual males than for their heterosexual counterparts. Christine Flynn Saulnier (1998) seeks to understand this reality through a review of the literature. She finds that these youths, as children or adolescents, are not equipped to manage ostracism, and their age often precludes their access to support systems more readily available to older individuals. Furthermore, most suicide attempts occur when youths either fear coming out or when they have just done so – often a time associated with personal and/or family crises. Unfortunately, professionals intervening in such situations too often view homosexuality as a phase, something that boys overcome.

As Flynn Saulnier points out, the studies tend to negate the existence of a general link between a homosexual orientation and psychopathologies. The psychological problems of homosexual individuals can be explained in large part by the highly heterosexist and homophobic environment in which they find themselves. Their problems most often result from fear, ostracism, and lack of contact with others like themselves. Further, their emotional and sexual desires are often denied or misunderstood, as is less but still commonly the case for heterosexual adolescents. When desires violate the norms, however, the ensuing problems are compounded. Young gay men are frequently rejected by their families and end up on the streets, where they are exposed to various abuses including rape and other forms of violence. Their lack of control and vulnerability is exacerbated.

Pierre Tremblay (2000) presents a comprehensive analysis of suicide problems experienced by young homosexual and bisexual males. He reports that "being gay" as an identity and the belief that sexual orientation is binary (one is either homosexual or heterosexual) are recent social inventions. Male homosexuality as conduct was common in earlier centuries, as Kinsey reported in 1948 and more recent researchers of western male homosexuality have found. Today the common (but unproven) belief that homosexuality may have biological causes (thus representing only a small percentage of the population) implies that most boys with recognized same-sex desires feel very alone.

They believe that they form such a tiny minority that no one – or almost no one else – in their immediate environment could be like them. This outcome is exacerbated by the fact that others have acquired the same beliefs and respond accordingly towards individuals known or suspected to be homosexuals. They are perceived to be "freaks."

In addition, because these boys are in violation of the hegemonic, socially specified "male role," underpinned by the belief that males should desire only females, the resulting perception – that a male who desires males must therefore be "like a female" – enters into the socially constructed situation. Boys blatantly violating gender role expectations with "feminine" behaviours are deemed anomalous, and they are accordingly abused and marginalized from an early age. In later years the stigmatization increases when the same attributes are equated with homosexuality. The fallout of this intersection of sexism, effeminophobia (the hatred of feminine attributes in males), and homophobia is elevated rates of suicidal behaviour for these marginalized males. Not only are they made to feel alone, isolated, deviant, and even freakish but the reaction in their immediate family and school environments will confirm their socially induced negative self-perceptions. They are in violation of social "real male" expectations in a world that has traditionally valued everything "male" as opposed to what is "female."

Furthermore, when these boys venture into gay communities, they soon discover that there too similar beliefs prevail. There too higher value is placed on so-called "real males," to the point that the most stereotypical masculine attributes are overvalued. In such environments, more feminine males may find themselves again marginalized in such a way that their suicide problems may be ongoing instead of resolved. In summation, a review of the literature indicates that not only are young homosexual males at risk for experiencing suicide problems but the more feminine of these males are at higher risk.

This brief sociological review permits us to construct a conceptualization of the problem, thus representing the biases and/or wisdom that are a part of the analysis and interpretation of the study data. Given the exploratory nature of our study, we now turn to the life stories of our study subjects, not to confirm or disprove any theory but rather to know and understand their perspective on the situation. Above and beyond the personal aspects of the stories specific to each individual, our sociological endeavour is focused on identifying common elements in their lives, but also their differences. Our objective is to describe how the lives of young homosexual males – or males identified as such – could result in states of mind where suicide becomes the only option.

3

The Young Men Studied

Who are our study subjects? First, they are volunteers, and in most cases their decision to contact us occurred in response to our advertisement for "volunteers" in newspapers and on bulletin boards of community organizations. Many respondees were refused because they did not meet the selection criteria. They were to be male, eighteen to thirty-five years of age when interviewed, and they were to have attempted suicide between the ages of fourteen and twenty-five years. In addition, their suicide attempts were to have resulted in their receiving physical and/or psychological care, and two years were to have elapsed since the last suicide attempt.

The initial sample consisted of thirty-two young men who had attempted suicide at least once. Twenty-four self-identified as homosexual, and eight identified as heterosexual.* None self-identified as bisexual, though many reported having had sexual experiences with members of both sexes. In the group of heterosexual males, one individual reported having always been

___

* With the aim of comparison, another group of eight gay males who had not made suicide attempts was selected towards the end of this study, especially to explore the resiliency factors reported in chapter 7.

identified as homosexual by others and treated accordingly, thus making his life more like that of the young homosexual males. Half of the homosexual males grew up in cities, eight were from small towns or villages, and five had lived in rural areas. Half of heterosexual males had grown up in cities, and the other half were from rural areas.

All study subjects were met individually. Their mean age when interviewed was 28.5 years for homosexual males and 26.8 years for heterosexual males, producing a mean age of about 28 years for the study sample. The mean number of suicide attempts was between two and three for both groups. The first episodes of suicidal ideation occurred between the ages of eleven and eighteen for most respondents, independent of their sexual orientation, producing a mean age of about fifteen years. The mean age for the first suicide attempt was the same for both groups: seventeen years. Although the age range for the first suicide attempt was eleven to twenty-five years, two-thirds of first suicide attempts had occurred between the ages of fourteen and eighteen.

Two-thirds of the respondents (n = 21) had some psychotherapy during their lives, and the mean age for the first such experience was 21.4 years and 25.0 years for homosexual and heterosexual males respectively. None had been in regular therapy before the first suicide attempt. As the result of a crisis, one-quarter of homosexual males had experienced living away from home in places such as a hospital or crisis centre. The same applied to half of the heterosexual males. In general, these experiences had occurred after the suicide attempt(s).

Many of those studied had a history of drug and/or alcohol problems. Eleven out of twenty-four homosexual males reported having been frequent users and abusers of these substances at some point in their lives. Seven out of the eight heterosexual males were also in this category. For the majority, drugs and alcohol were used to escape from their problems or to anaesthetize themselves in an effort to reduce anxiety.

Generally, these males had problematic or difficult relationships with their fathers. This was the case for twenty out of the twenty-four homosexual males and for five out of eight heterosexual males. Homosexual males, therefore, had no monopoly in this respect, and the same applied to relationships with their mothers. Only one-third of the homosexual males (eight out of twenty-four) reported always having had a positive relationship with their mothers, and only half of the heterosexual males (four out of eight). Two homosexual males and three heterosexual males reported that during their childhood or adolescence their mothers had committed suicide.

More than half of the homosexual males had at least one brother, and four reported having very negative relationships with their brother(s). Seven of the eight heterosexual males reported having brothers, none reporting having had negative relationships with them. One-third of homosexual males and five out of eight heterosexual males reported having sisters, and only one heterosexual male reported a negative relationship with a sister. About one-third of homosexual respondents (nine out of twenty-four) and one-quarter of the heterosexual males (two out of eight) reported having had strained relationships with their families. Overall, homosexual males reported having had more strained relationships with males in their families compared to females.

With respect to same-sex friendships, about three-quarters of the homosexual males (seventeen out of twenty-four) reported having had male friends, and the same proportion applied for heterosexual males, but a greater proportion of homosexual males reported friendships with females. On the other hand, heterosexual males (five out of eight) more often reported having been part of youth gangs, while few homosexual males (two out of twenty-four) reported such affiliations, thus making gang-related peer associations uncommon for the young homosexual males.

The males in the study attempted suicide in many ways. The most frequent were poisonings via overdoses with one or more medications, or via the use of toxic substances, accounting for about two-thirds of the attempts. Fourteen of the homosexual males attempted suicide in other ways, three by using car exhaust, two by hanging, two by slashing their veins, one by jumping from a bridge, one by purposefully contracting HIV, and one by repeatedly attempting suicide in a number of ways. Five of the heterosexual males attempted to end their lives via overdoses or poisoning, two by hanging, and one by slashing his veins. Some individuals in both groups repeatedly used the same method in their attempts to end their lives.

Half of the homosexual respondents had attended university, while only one of the heterosexual males reported having any post-secondary education. It is in this respect that our study subjects were the most dissimilar, but these differences would not be deemed statistically significant given the small size of the study sample.

Seven homosexual males (29.2 per cent) reported having been sexually abused by a man during their childhood or adolescence, as did two of the eight (25 per cent) heterosexual males.** By the time of their first suicide attempt, the majority of the young ho-

***

** These proportions are above the average reported for large North American studies which nonetheless estimate that 16 per cent of males have been sexually abused (Dorais 2002). Victims of sexual abuse are also reported to be at greater risk for suicide (Bagley and Tremblay 1997), meaning that a sample of male suicide attempters would likely have an over-representation of males who report having been sexually abused.

mosexual males had related sexually with a same-gender partner, and all the heterosexual males had related sexually with at least one female before their first suicide attempt.

Most of the homosexual respondents (twenty out of twenty-four) had lived or attempted to live a double life during at least a part of their lives; this involved hiding their homosexual orientation. The same number reported having perceived themselves negatively and having feared others knowing about their sexual orientation. Only three were accepting of their orientation when their first suicide attempt occurred. Twenty (83 per cent) reported that their attempting suicide was directly linked to their sexual orientation. For heterosexual males, no such link existed, but one of these males reported that his suicide attempt was linked to others perceiving him to be homosexual. All heterosexual males reported having had a negative self-perception but, unlike the homosexual males, they gave varied reasons for having negative self-images. These included problems with a partner, previous abuse, family problems, debt problems, and overuse of drugs. Finally, three homosexual males (12 per cent) reported having experienced a major depression before their suicide attempt(s), as did three heterosexual males (38 per cent).

We now proceed to the final part of the sample description, outlining the contexts, motives, and precipitating factors associated with the suicide attempts of the young men studied. For the majority of homosexual respondents, an important motivation for ending their lives was the rejection of their sexual orientation, and this was expressed in a number of ways: rejections from the social environment, moral harassment, related violence, and pressure to become heterosexual. At the more personal level, they experienced non-acceptance of their homosexuality, guilt related to having such desires, and the conviction that they could never be happy as homosexual.

Among the more immediate precipitating factors, moral harassment or bullying which had become unbearable was significant; the same applied to parental rejection. The revelation of homosexual orientation to the individual himself and/or to others was also significant, as was exhaustion from living a life of silence and solitude. In a few cases, deception in love or a terminated relationship compounded problems.

For heterosexual males, the stories were very different. Sexual orientation issues appeared to be unrelated to suicide attempts. The most commonly cited precipitating factors were family problems or the end of a love relationship, sometimes associated with depression or drug abuse.

4

Two Profiles, Four Scenarios

The young homosexual males in our study form two sub-groups: *early-identified* and *later-identified* boys. The early-identified males were pegged as homosexual between the ages of six and fourteen. In these cases, peers and other individuals had presumed they were homosexual on the basis of physical and psychological male stereotypes, such as not being good in sports and especially being "feminine." These males did not know exactly how they began to be identified as homosexual. Their stories also reveal, with respect to homosexuality issues, that intolerance reigns supreme in elementary schools, thus indicating that boys become conscious of such "differences" at a very young age. One young man reports,

At the age of six, I was being called a fag. I was already the school fag. Others therefore knew what I was before I did, even if at that time I understood none of this. Now, however, I understand. I knew I was different when my older brother got married. I was nine years old at the time. He was the first who was leaving the family, and I was sad because he was leaving, even though I did not have much contact with him; he was ten years older than me. To console me, my mother said that I too would one day meet a woman, get married, and leave home. Within me, however, I was thinking, it will not turn out this way for me! There was something strange to me in all this, but I did not know what it was. I could not ever see myself with a woman.

Most people believe that distinct groups of behaviours known as gender stereotypes exist for girls and for boys. Boys who are somewhat "feminine" become the victims of effeminophobia at an early age. This phenomenon essentially reflects a form of sexism. In our culture, feminine attributes in males are associated with homosexuality. It is therefore on the basis of such reasoning that a "feminine" boy will be identified, correctly or incorrectly, as homosexual. The designation will be accompanied by stigmatization.

Speaking about the responses of other boys to him, Marc recalls "only rejection."

Children are very mean. I don't remember their words anymore, but most of it was non-verbal. When I would approach others, they would move away. In winter when I would try to climb on a large pile of snow, they would push me down in a way that also told me that I was not wanted there. It was all very cruel. When it was time to be on a team, I was the last one picked. In fact, I was never chosen. A team inherited me like I was shit. Life was like this from primary school to high school. Courses in physical education were more like hell for me because I was always verbally abused. I was always so terrified of missing a shot that I would miss it, and all of this confirmed that I was really incapable.

A boy who gets along too well with girls and plays with them instead of playing with boys quickly becomes suspect, Serge reports: "They were calling me a fag because I played with girls at school. Because I did not play with boys." His efforts to gain his peers' acceptance were doomed to failure: "I didn't know what to do. I was alone because I did not like sports. I tried to play hockey on a team, but integration was impossible. I was not good enough."

Sylvain also felt excluded from the male group because of his gender nonconformity: "At school I was thought to be the black sheep, and it was the same at home, even if I was the only boy. Others found it odd that that I would play with girl dolls and not with trucks for boys. I was very quiet. Even the pre-school teacher at one point told my father that I would have problems sooner or later, given my interests."

Similarly, Louis was subjected to ostracism very early, beginning in primary school. Physical characteristics and a gentle personality, in his case, caused him to be perceived differently from others:

In primary school, they called me a fag because I had curly hair. I was shy and mild-mannered. The other boys said that I curled my hair, because I was a fag. I think that recurring statement somehow traumatized me. A gang of boys also greatly enjoyed calling me all kinds of names. They would chase me in the hallways. They would yell "Fag!" in front of everyone. In high school they would sit at the first table in the cafeteria and yell insults as I passed by. They would also let their wrists go limp.

To summarize, the boys we have called early-identified are pegged as homosexual and ostracized at a very young age, generally by the beginning of primary school. They are quickly placed in the role of scapegoat, and this status is difficult to bear because, in addition to the abuse, no one will come to their defence.

Later-identified boys, on the other hand, are deemed heterosexual and gender conformable (masculine) in their social environment and only later reveal themselves to be homosexual. This happens, often to the surprise of those who know them, near the end of adolescence or in early adulthood. For the later-identified, there is a "coming out," a public revelation to make, because their homosexuality has been kept hidden from family members, close friends, and peers. Their coming out is nonetheless generally preceded by a long period of fearing rejection. Martin recalls the reactions to his declaration that he was gay: "Returning from that weekend [he had visited a gay bar for the first time], I called all my friends, my parents, and my sister. It was a major coming out. However, I was scared that the girl I had been dating for some time would think I was scum. For my sister, it was a shock. For my mother, it was a big shock."

In spite of their apparently conforming nature, the later-identified males told us, as did the early-identified ones, that they had sensed a confusing "difference" between themselves and other boys since early childhood. Martin adds: "I always had the feeling that I was different when I was young, except that I did not accept it ... When I went out to a gay bar with my cousin, it all clicked."

Another respondent remembers becoming aware of his sexual orientation "around grade five. The others wanted to play BBQ tag [the game includes kissing girls] but I never wanted to play the game. I never wanted to play that game with girls. The first time I kissed a girl, I didn't find it exciting in any way."

For many males who later identify themselves as homosexual, their observations of the many abuses inflicted on those boys believed to be homosexual made them fearful and caused them to delay the affirmation of their sexual orientation. This confirms what Goffman (1964) emphasizes: the stigma has a way of spreading to anyone associating with the stigmatized. All boys somehow know this and recognize the risks. Christian's silence about his own homosexuality was very much related to witnessing the abuses inflicted on another boy pegged as gay: "At school, there was one boy who seemed to be homosexual. I was sure that he was gay. He had girls as friends but no male friends. He was called a fag and he was teased. Life was difficult for him. Seeing this didn't make me want to say, 'Me too, I'm gay.'"

Most boys know and understand that to be treated as a homosexual is the worst thing that could ever happen to them. However, boys identified as gay are not always homosexual. The labelling most often applies to gender-nonconformable boys. One respondent recalls being wrongly believed to be gay: "What I found so difficult was my femininity and my physical fragility. During all my adolescence, I was cruised by men and I was treated as a fag. I never had sexual desires for men. Others would say that I was a fag, and I did not even know what it meant."

FOUR SCENARIOS

Early-identified and later-identified boys develop different survival strategies that we call adaptive scenarios in response to rejection. As will become apparent, however, given the lack of evolution towards a positive outcome, most of these scenarios lead to dead ends. These scenarios are the Perfect Boy, the Token Fag, the Chameleon, and the Rebel.

The Perfect Boy

The Perfect Boy wishes to live up to expectations, and for him these are perceived more as commands. He wants and needs to be loved, meaning that he will not reveal his homosexuality to others, given the implied violation of heterosexual expectations. He will also strive for perfection in all ways. Most often he will be late-identified, and he will also be above suspicion, at least until proven otherwise. He prefers to be thought of as asexual. The Perfect Boy hides his stigmatized attributes, and he will seek to control his environment, as Goffman explains, and so will always present those parts of himself that will not result in stigmatization. His great fear is the anticipated embarrassing event that will compromise him. Jean-François's story illustrates this phenomenon.

"I had to be perfect. Nothing was ever enough," he often repeated when we met him. Jean-François is the youngest child in a family of three children. He has two sisters about fifteen years older than himself, one a dentist and the other a lawyer. His parents sent him to the best same-sex private schools because they did not want girls to distract him from his studies. He succeeded quite well academically, both at primary and secondary levels. He was always cheerful, with a sense of humour, and he was everyone's friend – the son any parent would wish to have. Homosexuality did not figure in his life plans, and he had relationships with females.

As time passed, however, the tensions increased. Under the mask Jean-François had constructed, he had increasing difficulty hiding his desires for other males. He was terrified that if he did not remain the ideal boy in the eyes of his family, he would be rejected forever. Disaster struck the day his mother discovered his diary, the only confidant of his emotions:

It was awful! I arrived from college one evening and my mother was crying on the sofa. Concerned, I approached her, but she pushed me away with her arm. She said, "I do not want to talk to you." I went to

my room and immediately saw that my diary was open on my desk ...
My father took it very badly ... He made attempts to have me cured.
He would have meetings at the table and try to convince me that I was
not gay, that it was all my imagination ... That moment marked the
beginning of the worst three years of my life.

After Jean-François's homosexual orientation was revealed, his
academic marks tumbled. Given that he felt responsible for his
parents' unhappiness, he was in free-fall. "It was total depression for me," he says. "I did not know what to do anymore. I
suffered enormously from the time that my parents discovered
I was gay. I had absolutely no will to live through that. My life
had ended, and I unable to do anything right, not at school or
anywhere else."

His parents became very cold towards him. They no longer
celebrated his birthday. Given his poor school performance,
they sent him to study in another city, but his marks remained
perilously low. He no longer had friends. Seeing no end or solution to his suffering, he decided to end his dilemma and its
related suffering by swallowing everything he found in his sister's medicine cabinet. Returning home early from a vacation,
she found him unconscious and took him to the hospital.

Sadly, Jean-François's story is typical of the accounts of other
respondents who played the role of the Perfect Boy to gain acceptance and also to be forgiven when their homosexual orientation became known. Another reports, "I was fearful of deceiving
my parents because I was their only son and, for them, having
descendants was very important. All my friends had girlfriends,
and compared to them, I didn't feel normal ... But I would try
not to let anything show."

Others adopted elevated ideals related to both masculinity
and sports performance as a way of compensating for being

gay. Patrice explains, "When you are effeminate, you're not a man. When you are a fag, you're not a man. A man is not any of that! A man is someone who is masculine, who is heterosexual. He is also good in sports. He's a guy who has muscles and a nice body and is athletic. Everybody also likes him, including other males. He has male friends, real ones ... That is what a man is."

Motivated by this leitmotif, Patrice became an accomplished athlete, and one resulting benefit was the sublimation of his desires. When he did act in accordance with his homosexual desires, however, he began asking himself how a champion like himself could have sunk so low. He was obsessed with the possibility that his secret would become widely known: "I was afraid of being harassed in the showers, and I was also afraid that the others would not want to have me on their team anymore."

According to these respondents, two tragic scenarios occurred when they could no longer play the role of the Perfect Boy.

First scenario: The young man reveals his homosexuality and the responses are disbelief, followed by the general dismay of all around him. He is perceived as a traitor and also as an intruder who has been lying about his real desires. He feels, with reason, that he is not understood, and that he is being judged and rejected. He then passes through a period of depression and attempts suicide: "I was trying to live up to demands, to live up to others' expectations. It was too much. It got to the point where all of this was no longer possible."

Second scenario: Instead of revealing his homosexuality, the young male attempts suicide so that he will take his secret with him and hide forever the desires perceived to be so shameful. "If my attempt to kill myself had succeeded, no one would have ever known that it was because of my homosexual orientation. My parents would have blamed it on family problems and on the break-up with my girlfriend."

The Token Fag

The person we have labelled the Token Fag is always early-identified because he is pegged as homosexual at an early age. At home, in public, and at school, he is the object of ridicule, harassment, and psychological and/or physical violence. Given the inaction of adults when faced with his abuse, he feels powerless in these situations, and he will sometimes consider his fate to have been sealed. (It is also possible that fear of stigma contagion is operating in the adults who do not try to protect the boy. Stigmatization by contagion, as explained by Goffman, is also possible beyond one's peer group.)

Hilaire's life story is typical of this scenario. The youngest in a family of four children, he recognized his sexual desires for other males around the age of fourteen. His peers, however, had thought him homosexual well before he recognized it himself: "When I was very young, some people laughed at me. They would call me a fag ... I already had effeminate behaviours, and I was not very masculine, that is true. I did not like to fight, and I did not like sports. All the boys despised me because of that."

Beginning in elementary school, he was terrorized by indiscriminate attacks: "Boys would often wait for me so that I would be caught in a trap like a mouse, and they would beat up on me," he recalls. "I wanted to be between the paint and the wall because I wanted to be invisible. I wanted to be invisible in hallways, in shopping malls – to be invisible everywhere because I was triggering this violence. I never knew when they would jump on me."

Hilaire believed he was wholly responsible for his problems: "The hatred and violence I was experiencing caused me to reject my sexual orientation even more. All of this also confirmed what I already knew: that I was a horrible human being. I would tell myself that I was a leper and that I must not accept my homosexuality. I hated myself so much as a fag!"

He did not seek help from adults, nor did he try to access resources at school or at home. He was afraid that the naming of things would create the possibility that they might be true. He was therefore silent, avoiding certain areas and making detours so that he did not encounter his harassers. Exhausted by the aggression he experienced, the chronic anxiety resulting from the fear of more aggression, and the lack of hope of ever having friends, he began to think of death as a liberation from the suffering he had endured since early childhood.

His young adult years began with an attempted conversion to heterosexuality. He met a girl with whom he lived as a couple for two years but eventually realized such a relationship was impossible for him. After this failure, he became depressed but still refused to accept his homosexuality. Perceiving suicide as the only answer to his suffering, he began to plan. He redirected the exhaust of his car so that he would fall asleep and die from carbon monoxide poisoning. However, after a few minutes he suddenly changed his mind and got out of the car before it was too late: "I experienced something like a nightmare. I saw my parents dealing with my death and decided that I could not do this to them. From that point on, I would not be choosing death as a solution to my problems."

While Hilaire stopped viewing suicide as a solution, Stephane attempted suicide many times. His story reveals other aspects of the problems often experienced by boys pegged as homosexual. He speaks of his childhood "in hell": "In primary and secondary school, I knew or felt that I was gay because I was always the scapegoat: the one who is abused – massacred – the most … It must be said that schools are very violent places, especially for anyone said to be queer or a fag. This was my situation. And my father also beat me. Nowhere was I sufficiently male, a man." For Stephane, it seemed normal to be ostracized and mistreated if one happened to be homosexual, and this conclusion reveals much about the social climate in which these children grow up. At a very early age, they quickly learn that expressions of violence are acceptable when directed at certain "unacceptable" individuals.

Serge's life story is similar. As the youngest in a family of three children, he was expected to follow in his brothers' footsteps, especially those of his eldest brother, the model son of the family. Serge wanted to emulate his perfect brother who was heterosexual and admired by all. However, something within him was different. Others also recognized "the difference," and they let him know in no uncertain terms that he was not living up to the prescribed ideal. He dreamed of being tall and masculine and having a military career. He perceived military life as the utmost representation of masculinity. "I wanted to be an American GI, to look like my older brother, and to be married with three or four children. For me, this would have been the perfect life." Serge's efforts, however, did not produce this outcome. He was too different.

Studious and intelligent, he did what he was told. He never fought with anyone; instead, he was often beaten up. Context was part of the problem: at the college that his brother had attended, others sensed his vulnerability, and he was therefore humiliated, rejected, and even assaulted. That was total failure. He nonetheless accepted his fate without complaining: "I was a fag, and a fag exists to be assaulted." At fourteen years of age he became discouraged because he could never be the desired ideal male, and he used his father's medication to attempt suicide.

The Chameleon

The Chameleon's self-perception varies from being one who pretends to be and at other times is an impostor. He plays at being heterosexual, or at presenting himself as heterosexual, in spite of his strong homosexual desires. He true identity is only discovered later, meaning that his early behaviour has prevented anyone from suspecting his homosexuality. The Chameleon can therefore play the role with few worries, at least at a young age, and especially before the pressures to conform and lie become too much to bear. This situation reaches crisis levels when he no longer wants to be a part of the masquerade that is suffocating him.

One respondent describes this double life:

I was more like an actor, and I acted the part for a long time, a very long time, right up to my final year at high school, to about the age of seventeen. When I told the truth to my girlfriend, she did not believe me. I resented not being able to be open in my relationships with guys, in the same way that guys can be with girls. I had to hide to be who I was, and that meant having sex with other guys in a car, in some deserted properties, or in the woods. I was hiding all the time, and that became unbearable. That is what kills.

At the time of the interviews, some respondents had not yet resolved the problem of revealing their more intimate lives to anyone, including those closest to them, even after their apparently "inexplicable" attempt(s) to kill themselves. One of the older respondents admits: "To this day, I keep lying to myself, and I also lie to those around me. When my friends want to introduce me to a girl, I always find an excuse to avoid such situations. I am still wearing a mask. Yet the desire to be real – authentic – is strong." He adds, "I am tired of lying, and it must all come out some day. If things get broken, so be it, except that I am now thirty-four years old, and I also have to live here."

It should not be concluded that the Chameleon is without courage. Arriving at a balance between his secret inner life and his everyday life is difficult for him, and the older he gets, the more he fails to see how to escape the situation. As a result, depression may set in and he may contemplate suicide, sometimes leading him to act to end his life. Christian led a chameleon life for years. He had a girlfriend for a while, and he was terrified of anyone discovering his secret: "I felt that I was human garbage because I was gay. I would have preferred telling others that I had AIDS to telling them I was gay. At least with AIDS, heterosexuals can have that. I also always believed that homosexuality was a disease, except that I considered AIDS to be more acceptable. I was a monster, someone who should not exist: human garbage."

As the result of his beliefs, Christian tried to convince himself that he could be heterosexual, that he could change his desires at will: "My friends knew nothing of this and suspected nothing. It was soon after a heterosexual relationship, when I was twenty-two or twenty-three years old, that I began to suspect that changing was maybe impossible. But I still could not accept myself, much less ever be able to tell my friends the truth." He used drugs and alcohol to handle the everyday pressures, including his self-acceptance problems. He also lived a clandestine sexuality, often relating with others like himself: "When I was stoned, I would forget all that … I would often meet the kind of man not known to be gay. One of them was a friend, and only I knew his secret. His parents knew nothing about this. I am not saying that this way of life is satisfying, or a healthy way to be. In his case, he had a girlfriend, and sex was something done quickly between the two of us." To end his self-rejection related problems, aggravated by the overuse of drugs (also confirming his failure in life), Christian attempted suicide using prescription drugs mixed with street drugs and alcohol.

Similar stories were reported by all the Chameleons we interviewed, but a few were more accepting of their sexual orientation. Their fear of being rejected, however, is initially much greater than their desire to be openly gay. When that balance shifts, the Chameleon's earlier success in disguising his sexual orientation may cause further problems with acceptance: "It took some time before I was able to be honest with people close to me, and especially with my relatives and immediate family. It took a good two years to do that. It's also as the result of a death in the family that I decided to be more honest. At the beginning, when I would talk about these things with my family, the reaction was: 'No way! It's not possible! Not you!' Obviously, I had played the game all too well!"

For Denis, despite his mother being a lesbian, the anxiety resulting from the fear of rejection prevailed. In his case, he feared that his mother would be accused of having "converted" him, which is exactly what his father did. Denis also knew what his mother had to live through as the result of her coming out, and he was afraid of experiencing the same social integration problems because of his homosexuality: "When I was young, it didn't worry me that my mother was lesbian, but the situation began to change when I was thirteen or fourteen years old. I would not bring anyone home anymore. When I discovered that I was gay, I would tell myself: 'If she, my mother, went through all that, I do not want to go through the same thing, that's for sure.' This was the source of much anger, and I would not tell anyone that I was gay because of this."

A Chameleon lives a double life, and he judges himself as not authentic. Some respondents have felt like hypocrites in their families and with their friends and colleagues. They often feel they are liars, impostors. They greatly fear being unmasked. For them, therefore, suicide means no longer living a lie. One respondent told us that he saw suicide as "the end of the problems. The end of the lies. The end of the headaches." Basically, Chameleons never feel comfortable in any situation. If they are acting like heterosexual males, they feel inauthentic, and they feel themselves to be dishonest, especially with their female partners. If they have clandestine homosexual relationships, they experience great guilt and become especially anxious about the possibility that their secret will become known. These boys may even assume an attitude of homophobia, given that it will help to dissipate others' suspicions about them.

The Rebel

Very few cases in the study group were identified as in the Rebel category because such individuals reject homophobia and develop a resistance that protects them in some ways from depression or suicide ideation. Jean-Michel's history is eloquent in this respect. Coming from a middle-class background, he is homosexual and has little difficulty accepting it. The same cannot be said for those around him: "I always was homosexual. I had no problems with that. I had difficulties, however, with being treated as a fag and with being pointed at. Children are tough and I was beaten up a lot, either by the other boys, or by my father."

Jean-Michel recognized that he was being ostracized because he was not what others expected him to be. He therefore revolted against his environment, and especially against his father. Instead of turning his anger on himself, he directed it towards the cause of the injustices he experienced – his family:

"I made friends with people who were into drugs. By the age of twelve, I had my little gang. At home, image was of great importance. In front of people, nothing was to show. I was to pretend … I was no longer able to do this, and I revolted against my father. I had to get out of there. I even invented the lie that he had raped me, to make sure that someone else would take care of me."

After many disappointments with drugs – the world into which he had ventured – and four suicide attempts, Jean-Michel accepted help because his "solution" had become the problem. Now in treatment for addiction problems, he has come to terms with himself and found inner peace. His rebellion against his family and all traditional values was both beneficial – he always refused to believe he was unacceptable – and harmful, because the only alternative available to him involved the use and abuse of drugs. We can only regret, as he does himself, that a young man severed from his family was unable to find a constructive alternative.

It must be emphasized that a number of respondents adopted more than one adaptive scenario, sometimes together, but more often in succession. In summary, the four life situations described above preceded their suicide attempts.

The Perfect Boy does not accept his homosexuality or the related homophobia. He becomes a perfectionist, and he is more or less asexual so that the difference between him and others is minimized, at least in his mind. The Chameleon also does not accept his homosexuality, but he accepts to a certain degree the homophobia in his environment, and he will sometimes participate in homophobic abuses of others. This is why he ends up "playing the game" of living only a heterosexual life, of wearing a mask for as long as possible. As for the Token Fag, he rejects his homosexuality because of the resulting prob-

Table 2   Four scenarios

Scenarios	Homosexuality	Homophobia
The Perfect Boy	refused	refused
The Chamelion	refused	accepted
The Token Fag	accepted/ sometimes refused	accepted/ sometimes refused
The Rebel	accepted	refused

lems, and he often accepts the homophobia oppressing him via its internalization, with significant resultant self-esteem problems. Finally, the Rebel accepts his homosexuality and does not accept the homophobia. This is the response least associated with suicide problems, possibly accounting for the rarity of such males in our study. The four scenarios are represented in the table above.

In summation, on the basis of their responses (and also in part on the basis of environmental responses) to their homosexuality on one hand and to homophobia on the other hand, the young homosexual men interviewed adopted different life scripts or scenarios. Their problems varied but were recurring because of the traps embodied within each scenario.

5

Life Situations

Four life situations played major roles in the problems that study subjects experienced around their sexual orientation, suicidal ideation, and suicide attempts. These include the family, schools, social environments where these young men were growing up, and social representations of homosexuality, especially in the media.

FAMILIES: BECOMING A STRANGER IN ONE'S OWN HOME

All homosexual respondents reported always having anticipated reprimands by members of their immediate or extended family. The repeated messages related to homosexuality heard since early childhood caused them to believe that homosexuality is the worst thing that could ever happen to anyone, and especially to a member of their family. This belief provokes the fear of abandonment in boys who are recognizing their homosexual orientation, and indeed parents often react very negatively when learning about their sons' homosexual orientation. Lack of support and resources needed to get through such a crisis may contribute to a youth becoming suicidal. The young homosexual males in this study left the family home earlier than their heterosexual siblings. We could say, in fact, that they were fleeing family homes where they had been silenced, made invisible and, at times, even ostracized. In contrast with their brothers and sisters who leave home with the blessings of all (for example, when a marriage occurs), young homosexual men receive no encouragement at their voluntary or involuntary departure. For some respondents, the revelation of homosexuality causes a major family crisis, resulting in the expulsion of the young men from their homes.

Some youths, and especially the Chameleons and the Perfect Boys, greatly fear such a dramatic outcome, which explains their long delay in revealing their homosexual orientation. In fact, many of our study subjects had not yet done this, although they were planning it. Even for the early-identified, already suspected of being gay by family members, the fear of a formal coming out is ever present. It seems that, for as long as nothing specific is said, the family can maintain the heterosexual image of their son.

Even for those who assert that their families are loving in nature, the fear of rejection is still present. It was therefore in this family climate of disguises, and often because of it, that many of the homosexual respondents fled their childhood homes. Revealing their homosexuality, they believed, would mean destroying a family ideal. Would they be forgiven?

Listen to one of our respondents:

Given my homosexuality, I lost the illusion that I could ever live normally, have children, be accepted by my family, walk hand in hand on the street, and publicly kiss the one I love. The dream of social integration died. I have a family who loves me, people who love me, and

I am too afraid to lose them because of this. I am escaping so that I can live my life. My family does not know I am gay. Maybe they suspect it, but they don't know for sure. I must tell them, I know. But if I had a lover, I would never tell them. I would keep that to myself.

The reported inner solitude has a great effect on the vulnerability of young gay men; they cannot depend on their families or, at least, most do not believe this is possible. Furthermore, when they are young, they are also unlikely to have the network of friends or acquaintances (sometimes called a "chosen family") needed to replace what is denied them.

A few respondents, like Claude, did reveal the more intimate side of themselves with the hope of still being accepted. But the outcome was very negative:

I left my parents' home at the age of sixteen because nothing was going well. I was experiencing one depression on top of other depressions, one suicide attempt on top of others. I could not stay there anymore. Communication was non-existent; it was like living on two different planets. In the end, living there was like living in hell. I tried to make them understand, but I was not able to say two words. As soon as I opened my mouth to talk about my sexual orientation, I was sent spinning. I was immediately degraded and no one wanted to hear any of this. For them, it was final: I was the bad one, the one on the wrong path. They were the righteous ones, probably as the result of the religious convictions they had at the time.

Like several other males interviewed, Claude found himself on the street with only the clothes he was wearing. Given that his friends were unaware of his homosexuality and that some were very homophobic, seeking help from them was not possible. It was therefore in silence, destitution, and solitude that he began to cope with family rejection. For him, and for most of the other young men studied, death soon enough presented itself as the only solution.

For the parents of the early-identified, the revelation of their son's homosexuality may be less difficult because the indicators have been present from an early age. This knowledge often causes parents to consider the likely outcome and, usually with some resignation, to foresee accepting that their son is gay. For them, such a revelation is more like a confirmation of their suspicions. However, even these parents rarely suspect and much less understand the highly problematic situations being imposed on their son. Out of shame, he does not speak about his problem; he is not the boy he was expected to be.

Like other early-identified boys, Hilaire was silent about his victimization. As a result of the assumptions that others made about his homosexuality, he was abused at school, and he was ashamed to be "like that." He was, in fact, too ashamed to talk about the situation and ask for help: "I was thirty-one years old when my parents finally learned about the violence I was subjected to in college," he says. "It was a shock for them. I had always remained silent about it."

Even when they suspect it, many parents seem to fear naming the problem, perhaps because they think they may be encouraging their son's homosexuality or because they are ashamed of having a homosexual son. The attitude of the father also seems to play a definitive role in the youth's desperation. For early-identified and later-identified homosexual boys, their father's approval is most important. They fear not living up to their father's expectations, and they especially fear his rejection. They want to please him and they want his reassurance and support. Unfortunately, aggressive, autocratic, or alcoholic fathers were not a rarity in this study.

Marc spoke to us about how his father's attitude contributed to his very negative self-image, and how in turn this contributed to his wishing to end his life:

The only male models I had were men who were suffering. My mother's brother always lived in our home, and he would drink a forty-ounce bottle of gin a week. My father and my uncles were violent, and they would laugh at me because I was effeminate. I was always afraid of my father who was stern and cold. I was brought up between two cases of beer. On my seventeenth birthday, he asked me to leave the house ... My mother would talk to him and he would come to see me later and apologize, but then the same thing would happen again.

The respondents' relationships with their mothers were generally not much better. The loss of the support and love of their mother may have serious consequences for boys, including suicidal ideation. If their own mother does not understand, who ever will?

For example, in Steve's case it was his mother who turned against him, telling him to get out of the house and her life:

My mother, I saw her as a saint. It was my mother who supplied all the affection at home. She did her duty as a mother, as dictated by her strong Catholic beliefs. I changed my mind about her, however, when I realized how stubborn she was. One day when we learned that a neighbour's son was gay, she said that if the same ever applied to one of her sons, she would never forgive him. She emphasized that she would have given life to the boy and she could take it away. Years later, around the age of sixteen, when I told her that I was questioning the possibility of being gay, she said: "You better leave now. I don't ever want to see you again." It's not easy at sixteen to find yourself alone and having to somehow survive. I will always remember that.

I worked as a delivery boy for a corner store. For at least a year I somehow managed to continue going to school, but only with great difficulties. I also lived in a real dumpy place. It was there that my first suicide attempt occurred. Two weeks after the death of my mother, I made a second attempt to kill myself. I had seen my mother on her deathbed and she said that she forgave me and that she was hoping for my cure – as if it was me who had to be forgiven for something and not her. When she died, I wrote a letter and placed a copy in her grave. I wrote that I forgave her and that I had missed her a lot. That, instead of holding me in her arms when I needed it, she had rejected me.

The same eloquence characterizes Guillaume's story. For his very rigid father, everything in his children's lives was expected to eventually turn out in a specified way: career, marriage, and so on. Guillaume's childhood was therefore more like military training. He was sent away to private schools chosen by his father: "I was boarding in the best private schools; at least this was what I was often told. Yet I was sexually abused by doctors and also by priests in one college where I lived. I was raped anally and subjected to other forms of sexual violence for years."

When his father learned the unacceptable truths about his son, he threw Guillaume out of his home. Guillaume was sixteen years old at the time, and he went to the United States where he began working as a prostitute so that he could survive: "For six years I travelled throughout North America without giving anyone any news about me. There were many hardships, but I eventually overcame them. I had a difficult life, but I owe nothing to anyone."

Guillaume got married and became the father of the child he is caring for today. During those early years, however, he used drugs and alcohol heavily and had sex with numerous men, all done as if there were no tomorrow. He consciously adopted unsafe sex practices and injected drugs, knowing the syringes could be contaminated with infected blood. For him, this was a way to end his life:

I had given everything I had, and I was tired of living. I abused alcohol, and it was the same with sex. I was feeling alone, even if people were around me. I could not see a light at the end of the tunnel and I therefore put everything in order for my great departure. My sexual orientation is not a factor in my attempts to kill myself. That was related to my father's behaviour and his rejection of me. By the end of my adolescence, I worked on a ski patrol. It was there that I made my best friends. Nobody knew I had homosexual tendencies. It was not written on my forehead and I was appreciated, but I was alone.

Sometimes brothers added to the problems being experienced with parents. One respondent reported that it was his eldest brother who sexually initiated him by forcing sex on him, who outed him to the family when he decided to live his homosexuality at the end of his adolescence. Here it must again be noted that our respondents experienced elevated rates of childhood sexual abuse, most often by family members, thus making it an important risk factor, as reported in the previously cited Omega Cohort study (Otis et al. 2000) and by Bagley and Tremblay (1997). In the latter quantitative study, males who had been sexually abused before the age of sixteen years were more likely to have had suicide problems including actual attempts.

Denis's story may seem exceptional, but it illustrates how, even for those who knew they would receive support from family members, the public revelation of their homosexuality was still problematic:

My mother is lesbian, and she accepted very well the fact that I was homosexual. On the other hand, my father does not speak to me anymore. My sisters had suspected that I was gay and took it well. Yet up to the end of my adolescence I was ashamed. I did not want to be like that. I had seen what my mother had to go through to accept herself and to be accepted by others, and I did not want to also go through that. My father had been very angry with her, and he was even more resentful when he heard about me. Some people reproached my mother for having somehow influenced me. My father said that it was because she was lesbian that his son was gay, and that was hurtful. For me there is no relationship between the two. My sisters are not lesbians, yet my mother is lesbian.

My real problem was with my father. I often tried to speak with him, but it never amounted to anything. I then found myself a girlfriend and tried to cure myself. I went to see my father with her. I had become normal because there was my girlfriend to prove it. We even had a child together, and this caused my father to stop calling me a fuckin' faggot. It was when my relationship with this girl ended that I attempted suicide. I could not get to the point of abandoning my wish to be heterosexual … I had not yet come to grips with the evidence.

Some parents need time to adapt and, happily, they will eventually seek to understand their son. All stories do not end up being family dramas. A truly loving family will help the boy, sometimes *in extremis*, to accept himself as he is and to cope with ostracism:

They learned about me being gay after my suicide attempt. My sister's response was very positive. My brother-in-law's reaction was not so positive, but not extreme. As for my parents, my mother took the news not too badly. For my father, however, it took some time, but his response was most surprising. I was at their home in the country,

and one of his friends was there. He made a comment about me being gay and my father said: "Listen, this is my son. He is what he is
and I love him as he is. If all of this troubles you so much, there's the
door. This is my home and my son is in his home here, and I don't
want any comments on that." After that, I was always accepted and
with them things went quite well for me. Today, I am a central figure
in the family.

Obviously the family plays an important role in the evolution of young homosexual males in both positive and negative
ways. This applies to acceptance of self and self-esteem and to
their desire to live. A rejection by the family, especially if it appears final, can play a major role in a young man's decision to
end his life. Conversely, a climate of understanding and acceptance can help a boy overcome suicidal thoughts and the belief
that his being gay will certainly result in his rejection by the
family, meaning the loss of those most dear to him: his father,
mother, brothers, sisters, and so on.

SCHOOLS: THE LEARNING OF HATRED

For our respondents, schools were places of harassment. Abuse
most often took a psychological form, but physical violence was
also very common. At school, the boy pegged as homosexual or
deemed to be insufficiently masculine risks being tormented by
other boys. Worse, he will not get support from his peers, from
teachers, or from his family. Even those boys who remain invisible, the ones we have called later-identified, will be living in
fear. They dread the discovery of their secret because they believe this will cause them to suffer the same fate as boys known
or suspected to be gay, the ones called early-identified. These
closeted boys may also be homophobic, especially when it is required to dispel possible suspicions of their homosexuality.

The adolescent years are supposed to be the best of one's life. For young males labelled as homosexual, these years are often the darkest. Marc recalls this time as a long period of painful isolation:

I felt alone, from primary school to high school. I did not hang out with any group of boys. Going to a dance with the heterosexual gang was not something I wanted to do. I was looking for an identity, an anchor, but nothing presented itself. I did not feel like I belonged in my community, and the same situation existed at school. I felt like I was an outsider. I especially did not like physical education classes.

In primary school, kids can be very mean. I would play girls' games because that's what I liked to do. Automatically, I would then be called a fag.

Sylvain suffered greatly from being rejected at school, and like many others in our study, he quit school early:

From grade four to high school, the boys called me a fag. They would beat up on me, calling me every name imaginable, and they pushed me around. I was punched out a lot because I was a fag, especially by one guy, always the same one. I was unlucky: he was always in the courses I was taking. I would wake up in the morning and cry because I did not want to go to school. My mother did not understand, but how does one explain that? ... I finished my studies at a school for adults. Adults were more able to accept me. It was more open. At the end of secondary school, when people asked, "Why don't you have a girlfriend?" I would say, "It's because I prefer finishing my studies and having some money before I begin thinking of getting a girlfriend." I would not say, "I do not have a girlfriend because I am gay." I had found a way to avoid telling the truth, all because I wanted to be left in peace.

It is symptomatic that this young man, instead of thinking that the situation at school was unacceptable, attributed his fate to bad luck. Like most of those we called Token Fags, Sylvain had internalized the environmental homophobia to the point that he perceived it to be an unfortunate and un-avoidable fact of life.

Louis was also subjected to chronic harassment. His tor-mentors seemed to be motivated by both attraction and repul-sion. "I was harassed all the time I spent in high school," he recalls, "most often by the boys on the football team, and espe-cially in the locker room. They would flash themselves in front of me. They would put their ass in my face, in front of every-one, and they would all laugh. It got to the point that I did not want to take a shower because I was endlessly being harassed."

For many, physical-education courses are a living hell and the locker rooms and shower rooms nightmares. The boister-ousness and nudity in the locker rooms also add to the ho-mophobic tension. The Token Fag seems to exist to prop up the masculinity of others. It is not, however, only in the locker rooms that violent events occur. Hilaire reports on the con-stant threat he was made to feel at school:

Horrible things would happen every day, like being pushed into a locker "by accident." Like being kneed so that I would fall down with my tray full of food; all the cafeteria would then explode in laughter. I even almost got used to it. But in the week preceding my suicide at-tempt, I had been a victim of something quite violent. I had gone to the study room, a room with about one hundred desks, at the end of an afternoon. Not many students were there, and the supervisor was sitting in front of the room, talking with other students. A teacher was also there. Four guys came in through the back door and began to beat me up. They were kicking me and calling me a fag. No one – not the supervisor, not the teacher, nor any of the students there –

did anything about the situation. After that, I was convinced that I was less than nothing, that I was just a fag, and that I therefore deserved it! I also did not dare tell my parents what had happened because I was ashamed of the reason motivating the assault.

After this violent experience, certain that he was condemned to suffer such acts for his whole life, Hilaire couldn't take it any longer. He was worn out by daily life, and he was also angry with himself. Enraged because he could not do things as they should be done (including defend himself) and incapable of being what was demanded of him – not being homosexual – he looked desperately for a way out. A short time after the event in the study room he took advantage of his parents' two-week vacation to try to end his life, swallowing a bottle of his father's antidepressants. This was his first suicide attempt.

Sensing that they are more or less different than the others and being confused about this, some boys will seek to deflect attention by disruptive behavior. One young man recounts, "I was doing a lot of bad things, and I was suspended from school a number of times. I was never really aggressive or violent; it was more like an image created to avoid being abused. I had to look tough so that the guys would not suspect that I was a fag."

A few respondents reported having positive experiences in school, but these were rare. For example, one spoke of having had an openly gay teacher, which seems to have produced long-term positive effects.

I had a teacher who was gay. It was almost written on his forehead, and he did not care. At one point, the boys had written him an agressive letter. He spoke about it openly, saying to the class: "I am homosexual and I am quite comfortable being homosexual. If some of you have a problem with that, you can ask the school director to place you in another class. When I was hired, he knew about this, and so did your parents. You live with it, or leave." I placed that teacher on a pedestal, and I never stopped thinking about what had happened. It did a lot for me to know it was possible to have that kind of courage.

It is not by accident that the lives of young gay men are often difficult in schools, because homosexuality is widely ridiculed in most of these institutions. Furthermore, the few efforts made to sensitize students to homosexuality issues may be superficial and short lived. As Sylvain recalls, "When the nurse spoke about homosexuality, everyone began to laugh. I laughed with the others to avoid having them suspect that I might be homosexual."

In brief, for a young man who is gender nonconformable or presumed to be homosexual, schools generally continue to be dominated by indifference and hostility, and he will obtain little help or protection (see also Harris 1997). The resulting anxiety and violence, which is both physical and psychological, can contribute to depression and distress, followed by suicidal ideation. The most insidious and harmful experiences often occur when a youth complains to those in authority about being harassed and assaulted. Usually he is blamed for the problems; apparently he can only ignore those who are tormenting him, learn to be "discreet," or learn to defend himself! One respondent reported that the director of the school told him that it was his responsibility to not "provoke" others, apparently by being inconspicuous and therefore making others forget about him, and also by remaining unaffected by the slander and threats.

Some schools have avoided the recognition that homophobic violence is a collective problem, as has been recognized for abuses and violence related to sexism and racism. Blame is placed on the victim, instead of preventing such violence by intervening at the causal end of the problem. As a result of this unfortunate bias, young homosexual males and those identified as such by others are made to suffer even more, for they cannot foresee any solution to their misery.

In later years the workplace may also become a place of ongoing confrontation. Jean-Michel describes one such environment:

At work, the men treat each other as fags, and I first thought they were talking about me. One day I realized I had been wise to fear them. One of them said, while looking at me: "She forgot to wear her skirt this morning." From then on, it was endless. If I got angry, they would say that I was menstruating. Said once, it can be humorous, but after ten times, it's not so funny. Luckily, the boss intervened to calm things down. Men are so terrified of being thought of as fags if they are not anti-gay. There is nothing that I did not hear. They even said that fags should all be isolated somewhere and that they would then exterminate each other. How do you expect someone to keep a sense of humour or safety in a place like that?

NEIGHBOURHOODS:
EVER-PRESENT DANGERS

For the boy identified as homosexual, even the ordinary comings and goings of daily life can be stressful, because he never knows when and where he will be insulted, threatened, or assaulted. Homosexual or effeminate boys often feel that they are being tracked, and not without reason. Many report that certain places in schools are to be avoided, and the same applies for deserted streets and trails where violent acts can occur without the presence of witnesses. Given that these youths usually have few friends they can depend on, they are often alone and thus easy prey for anyone seeking to harm them. At a later age for some of these boys, the "gay ghetto" (such as the "Gay Village" of Montreal) will play an important role in reclaiming a safe territory perceived to be a place of liberation and protection.

However, for young men who are frightened that their homosexuality may be discovered, gay meeting places are too risky. Gaétan reports:

In the city where I grew up, everything is very, very closeted. I would go out to the bars, the straight bars obviously. There was a gay bar, but it was to be avoided if you didn't want to be identified. Yet I would still succeed in making contacts with older men. It's not easy, but there were always gay males in straight discos. At that time, ongoing relationships between two males did not exist for me. I would not go to the gay bar because I didn't want to be pointed at. I went once and I was very nervous, telling myself: "If ever someone …" No male who wanted to keep his reputation would ever have gone there.

Going to certain places may compromise a young man's reputation, and especially his sense of security. Heterosexual males can meet sex partners anywhere, but young gay males must do this circumspectly and live hidden lives, especially outside the larger cities where it is easier to maintain one's anonymity. This is why after their suicide attempt(s) many of the interviewed young men felt that they had to leave their rural or semi-rural homes and move to a large city. The desire to leave the past behind, along with the environments associated with it, increases with the realization of just how restricted are the spaces and times in which freedom may be experienced.

Gaétan continues, "When I began to fall in love with other guys, I could no longer stay at my mother's home. My lover would drive me home and we would kiss at the door, but we had to be careful that no one saw us. Yet, a neighbour did see us and my mother was told that she should not permit this, that the neighbours were troubled because her son was doing such filthy things at the door ... I understood."

In new territory in large cities, *real life* is possible. When we feel safe in an area, we seem to have more control over our lives, as one respondent concludes:

When I came to Montreal, I burned the bridges to my past because I had always sensed that I was living a double life. I closed the door to that life of living a lie. The gay discussion groups have permitted me to understand my relationship with myself. They permitted me to become completely self-asserting, to understand myself, and to also become social. For me, making contact with other gay people was quite easy because I knew someone at Lambda Youth.* When you don't know where to go, it's not easy. There's no doubt that being in Montreal helped a lot with my coming out. I am not sure that if I had been elsewhere, even in Quebec City, I would have had the opportunity and support that I received in Montreal. The gay community is large here. There are more opportunities to socialize and integrate in the gay world in Montreal, compared to other places.

Eric had to flee his family because his homosexuality was not accepted. He had become a stranger in his own home. He also had to quit school because his safety had become compro-

* Lambda Youth (Jeunesse Lambda) is a gay and lesbian youth group in Montreal. It provides services for young gay males and lesbians.

mised: "I lived a total war situation. I never knew when I would be assaulted." He became a street youth: "I escaped to Montreal to live a gay life. I slept in saunas and under balconies, and I frequented dangerous areas. I had nowhere to go. I was also having high-risk sex." Eric understood what it meant to not have a territory and not be at home anywhere. Instead of living on the streets, he was soon travelling throughout Canada in association with a youth project. On his return he did odd jobs and worked in mills and factories, but he did not feel comfortable anywhere. "It's awful what I ended up hearing," he says. "In places like that, in factories, homosexuality doesn't exist. In white-collar places and in universities, it's probably more like being in a gay colony ... In factories, it's macho. Guys grab each other's crotches, but it's always gross straight jokes. There's no place for gays there."

When Eric went to live in a gay area, he felt liberated: "The gay world, that's like a different universe. The bars are unique places where we can meet others like us. It is paradise for many." Unfortunately, young men who leave their villages for a gay village may find that it is not always as safe as they hoped, given that homophobic violence also occurs there. Yet many of the respondents found that venturing to live in gay areas was a positive turning point in their lives. In such places they had opportunities to meet others and felt reassured by being able to experience solidarity with others "like them."

Dominic grew up in the country, and his life story is typical of homosexual life in rural areas. As the eldest and only son in his family, he was expected to take over the land. In his family, farming had long been a tradition; the farm had been passed on from father to son for generations. There was also a sense of duty when it came to the land, to one's ancestors, and to future generations. Dominic panicked. He was smothering in the world imposed on him and was terrified of deceiving others. It was in the family barn, in fact, that he would seek to end his life by hanging himself.

I was born on the farm, in my parents' home. I live in an agricultural world, in the country, in a farming family where the land goes from father to son. In a world like that, homosexuality is something that belongs in the circus; it's not "people like us." I remember school trips when we were passing through the east side of Montreal and students would say: "Look! We are going to see some fags! That where the fags live!" Now imagine seeing me ever say that I am one of them. Anyway, I could not be like that. I could not identify with anything in the gay world, nor with anything being said about what it apparently was.

Another respondent who had to leave his small home town because of the prejudices found himself just as isolated in Montreal. He began using drugs to hide and forget what he calls his "problem": "I preferred being pegged as a drug user to being known as gay. The evenings with the family, the marriages, the outings – it all reminded me that I was not like the others." As this respondent indicates, there are many life situations where young homosexual males do not feel like they belong, when they are made to feel marginalized and abnormal. It is therefore unsurprising that such environments sometimes become suffocating, even leading to suicidal feelings and behaviours. When a youth feels that no place exists for him anywhere – or worse, that he will forever be watched and oppressed – the possibility is great that he will think of escaping his prison. He may go to a large anonymous city, if he can afford it, or he may decide to terminate his life. A large city may also not live up to expectations, meaning that some youth venturing there will have ongoing problems related to their homosexuality.

SOCIAL REPRESENTATIONS
OF HOMOSEXUALITY: SILENCE,
RIDICULE, AND INSULTS

The social representation dimension involves such media as newspapers, public discourses, magazines, films, radio, and television. These are the places of "we say," "the public believes that …" In this area we find the public images of homosexuality, influenced by politics, religion, and so on. Generally, the media presents few positive images of gay individuals. A respondent recalls: "We would listen to Janette[**] on television; the subject was homosexuality. My mother and father made some comments about homosexuals: they were perverts, and there was definitely something wrong with them. My family would also never accept a sick person like that in their home. I was crushed. I told myself: What's the use of living? That was the trigger."

The social environment willingly relays the popular stereotypes and prejudices: "Close to my home, there was the neighbour's son; his name was Pierre, but everyone called him Pierrette." A boy therefore quickly comes to understand that it would be in his best interest to hide any attribute resulting in such stigma and ostracism. In such environments, where homophobia is integrated and visible, exorcizing these negative images may be done via denial (possibly including becoming visibly homophobic) or escape (the over-use of drugs or alcohol, for example). Some, however, will act in accordance with feelings related to ending one's life, to be done as quickly as possible given the hopelessness of the situation.

[**] The first name of a famous talk-show host on Quebec television, Janette Bertrand.

Stephane explains how religious discourse contributed to his suicidal thoughts by continuously providing monstrous images of homosexuality:

I always saw the sin. My parents were fervent believers. For them, homosexuality was to be condemned. God rejected and hated gays. A god of love, so it seems. My parents always wanted to change me. I was the guilty one, the one who was no good, if I did not want to change, if I could not change. They would make me read stories of gays who had managed to change and also got married. I was a big monster, social garbage. If religion had not been there, I would have maybe not tried to kill myself. It was super oppressing, that idea of sin, abnormality, and blame, with everyone around me believing it.

Another respondent describes a similar problem around religious discourse: "Religion in general, whatever name it may have, says that if you are gay, you are going to hell; God hates fags. If you have a disease like AIDS, or if anything else happens to you, it's all a punishment by God. If this is infinite forgiveness, I wouldn't want to see divine vengeance! I was so traumatized by religion … I had to find alternatives. The time also came when, even though I still went to confession, I would place a limit on the sins I would confess."

It would seem that compatibility is impossible between religious beliefs and homosexuality for those interviewed young men who described themselves as believers, or as having been so. The journey to acceptance of being gay must pass through religious rejection, they say. It is the major issue: "For me, religious belief was something left behind at the age of eighteen or nineteen. Now, even to venture into a church twice a year would be extraordinary. I have developed my own faith. It is in everyday behaviours that one is charitable and good, not in practising a hypocritical religion. Homosexuality is banished from religion, so I have therefore banished religion."

Alexander tells us how homosexuality was perceived in his family. The references made in this case involved pornographic images in magazines and pathological characterizations in the press:

My father was quite liberal; for him, men were men, and he was proud to be a man and to have sons. When I was nine or ten years old, he showed me a *Playboy* magazine. The girls were naked, inviting. My father was showing them to me and saying: "A girl, is that. They are to be caressed and penetrated with your penis." But he never told me that two guys could do the same together. He never said anything about this, nothing for or against it.

My mother, on the other hand, we knew what she thought. For her, it was a major scene when we learned that a neighbour had caught her nineteen-year-old son in bed with another guy. Whenever newspapers reported a story related to sexuality, she always made it into something major. A paedophile had killed a boy, and she would say that it was a damn faggot who had done that. For her paedophilia was equal to homosexuality, which meant the rape of children. When I told her about myself, she said: "There's no one with a mental disorder in our home. You better quit that. What will people think?"

Homosexuality is always like an accusation. It is the worst insult you can use with another man. Didier Éribon (1999: 29) discusses the role of insults: "To begin with, there is insult. The one that a gay individual will hear at one time or other in his life will highlight the fact that he is psychologically and socially vulnerable." Almost all the respondents – and we must remember that eight of them were heterosexual – spoke to us about their fear of being homosexual, or of being thought to be homosexual, because the anticipated public responses were always very negative.

The majority of homosexual respondents, and especially the early-identified, lived with recurring situations in which they were publicly insulted. These insults took many forms, ranging from the ridiculous to the insidious to the blatant. Most often their objective seemed to be to serve as a warning to all, not just those young men who are or could be homosexual, that punishment would result if they stepped out of line. Because of the abuse inflicted on the early-identified, the daily victims of insults, the later-identified often delayed their self-affirmation, fearing that they too would be humiliated in the same way:

When the guys wanted to hassle another guy, they only had to say he was a fag. I was so afraid to be endlessly bothered with that! It's a subject that no one dares speak about too much. Heterosexual males often endlessly harass others that way, mostly to humiliate them. I'd tell myself that in the locker room, if ever anyone knew about my homosexuality, it would not be pretty ... I would hear boys talk a lot: when they saw gays on television, they would pretend to be puking.

Even as adults, many of the respondents felt targeted by others at the slightest hint that they might be homosexual. Any public display of affection could be censured: "We were at the hospital's Emergency after my last suicide attempt. I was with a friend who was holding me in his arms because I was hurting so much. Some nurses told us, 'Be discreet, because you are disturbing the sick people here!' I felt like leaving."

The social image of homosexuality is constructed on the basis of what is presented – and what is permitted to be visible –

about that reality. According to many respondents, the media
has helped little in terms of helping the public to evolve. One
respondent spoke about television and radio as places where
the most conservative homosexual prejudices and stereotypes
have, until very recently, too often been perpetuated: "I'm not
able anymore to tolerate the dumb fag jokes we hear on television variety programs, or the nonsense sometimes heard on the
radio. There's no way that those people could ever say the
same things about black people, and even less about Jews,
without having their knuckles rapped. Me, I'm insulted, and
especially because after hearing these dumb jokes I hear them
repeated by others. It's not easy to live with that."

Another respondent elaborates:

In the 1980s, there were few gays on television. It's partly for that reason that I felt so alone in the world, and so different from others. Today, it's almost like every TV soap has its gay person, but their only
role is to be gay, nothing else, really! We almost never see gays living
their lives like we see heteros do, like seeing them kissing, touching
each other, living a love life and even an erotic one. Gays on TV, they
have to look neutral. Or they have to be a like a circus act. I remember an ongoing program in which there was an effeminate male, the
ultimate fag – which affected me very negatively.

Of course, there was the famous film *Philadelphia*, which I saw
seven times. My parents did not yet know about me, but I did. I
brought my parents to see the film, given that I had told them how
much I liked it. In a world where there were few positive images
available to me, I would say that for me that film had a positive effect
on my self-acceptance. It was telling me that homosexuality existed
and that there were people in the world I could identify with. Even if
on the personal side the gay characters were not well developed, this
was getting close to what I was and to what I wanted to be …

To listen to someone say, "Oh, this actor is the fag in that program!" or something like that really affected me negatively. I would become sad, even feeling a little attacked. It troubled me to hear people say "It's the fag," because it reduces all gay people to one thing. I hadn't yet told myself that I was homosexual, or fully accepted that I was, and I was feeling that these things were being said to stop me from being gay.

Public representations of homosexuality evidently had a significant influence on some respondents who generally deplored the paucity of gay role models available to them. When silence prevails about homosexuality in families and in schools, we should not be surprised that media such as television, radio, or films will represent a venue via which young homosexual individuals will desperately seek models and information – something to give them hope.

6

Isolation, Shame, and Stigmatization

So far we have looked at the day-to-day risks, misfortunes, and traumatic events experienced by the twenty-four young homosexual men in our study. One important question asked of respondents related specifically to the circumstances leading to their suicide attempts. Two life situations were significant, and the more important was the exhaustion and hopelessness linked to the psychological (and sometimes physical) isolation most of them experienced. This followed the pattern of sensing themselves to be "different" from others from an early age, feeling the social inducement of shame in relation to their "difference," and fearing the real or anticipated stigmatization associated with this "difference," their recognition of their same-sex desires. The second factor, experienced in most cases, was that there was no one with whom they could discuss their distressing problems, and none of the help, support, and encouragement they needed to develop any hope for a future less bleak than the one they anticipated.

For the eight heterosexual respondents, suicidal periods were generally related to the experience of unforeseen events, such as a break-up with a girlfriend. In these situations, however, they knew their problems could be revealed to others; it was possible for them to ask for help, even though this avenue may have been precluded by a depression-related withdrawal from the world. Their suicide attempts were also not associated with a redefinition of self as was the case for most homosexual males who were experiencing an anxiety-ridden and anguished period of self-questioning. For this latter group, their identities were at issue, with the implication being "I am homosexual. I am not like others." Their lives were about to become greatly restricted by either revealing or hiding this intimate and important part of self. In addition, the moral harassment that many respondents experienced generally negated the possibility or even the right to be helped by others because these youth felt they had been discredited. Boris Cyrulnik (1999: 65) asks, "Acute traumas are debilitating, but do they have more lasting effects than the never-ending stress that becomes imbedded in one's memory and modifies one's emotions, knowledge, and perception of self?"

The young homosexual male respondents differed from their heterosexual counterparts in other important ways. Young gay men did not know who to turn to for understanding and help. They feared being rejected by the people apparently available to guide them through life's difficulties: their parents, teachers, religious leaders, and so on. Their doubled burden therefore involved struggling with a serious problem and also feeling that it was impossible for anyone to understand and help them. This burden was a typical result of their victimization by moral harassment. Furthermore, young homosexual males are also often placed in the role of having to educate those around them after their coming out. In some cases it took months or even years before their parents stopped wanting them to "change."

Of particular significance was the common indifference manifested by family members, peers, and school authorities when these youth were subjected to psychological and physical violence. These commonly repeated experiences generally verified their conviction that nothing could be done about their situation, that no one would ever understand their problems, and especially that they could never expect help from anyone. One respondent spoke about the ostracism he experienced in college and a serious physical assault that took place in front of teachers who did nothing to help him. For this young man, it was less the violence of the other students than the indifference of those in authority, who should have protected and defended him, that led to his great distress and the attempt to end his life. He was ashamed of what had happened to him and ashamed of speaking about it; he was afraid of being blamed for the abuses by being defined as "not normal."

Some boys sought opportunities to speak of their problems with a family member, but they were quickly rejected; one was immediately thrown out of his home. They learned that silence was the best policy. When the people who are apparently available to help and protect us do nothing – or worse – they only add to the dilemma. Who then does one turn to? This is the question with no good answer that haunts many homosexual adolescents. For them, suicide seems to be the only way to "liberation." This was the expression many of them used to describe the dilemma of their situation. As one respondent concluded, "With suicide, it's the end of problems! The end of living in hell!"

The sense of isolation – of being alone – is experienced acutely but differently by the four categories of homosexual males identified in our study: the Perfect Boy, the Chameleon, the Token Fag, and the Rebel.

The Perfect Boy fears deceiving his family and friends, and he especially fears public opprobrium, given his desire to please everyone and (he hopes) to minimize the negative responses, should his homosexual secret be discovered. For good measure, he may also be asexual, with the hope that this neutral status will protect him from suspicion or rejection.

The Chameleon fears that his "impostor" status will be discovered, in spite of his having made great efforts to "pass" as straight. For this young man, it is crucial that his masculinity and heterosexuality status never be questioned, given that his constructed image is based on social expectations. Therefore, even within his family, or when he is accepted and popular with peers, he is obsessively troubled that his secret desires will be discovered and that his homosexuality will be known to all. One respondent recalls, "There was a guy who seemed to be gay and he was always harassed. So in the locker rooms I would always look at the floor to be sure that no one could ever accuse me of looking at the other guys' bodies." This youth illustrates what Howard Becker (1963) notes in his analysis of exclusion: one needs only to be suspected of a norm transgression to awaken doubt, to be ostracized and excluded. The boys often highly esteemed by others – those classified as the Perfect Boy and the Chameleon – experience an intense, ever-present inner anguish that their homosexual desires will be discovered and they will forever be rejected because of them.

Loneliness characterizes the Token Fag who has been the scapegoat since an early age; he is the one that most boys mock and refuse to play with or accept. The saying "Birds of a feather flock together" explains why most boys will avoid associating with the Token Fag; this is related to belief that stigma is contagious, noted by Irving Goffman (1964). Furthermore, given that such boys are rarely gifted in sports, their opportunities to socialize with peers become scarce. Such a boy therefore often believes himself to be unique, the only one of his species in the world, a feeling justified by his peers' decree that he represents all that a boy should not be, that he is a freak. His exclusion may also be reinforced by some boys sensing themselves to be similar, mostly because they fear that any association with him will result in the same abuses being directed them.

At a time in life – childhood and adolescence – when rejection or acceptance by one's peers is very important, when the first feelings of sexual attraction play a monumental role in our sense of relationship with others, the imposed fate of the Token Fag is exceptionally cruel. Without friends and especially without desired love relationships, these marginalized adolescents are living a loneliness that may seem impossible to overcome. Furthermore, within their families, uneasiness and silence often rule, and these boys experience varying degrees of rejection, especially by their fathers. Many parents are concerned and disapproving when a boy appears more "feminine" than "masculine" in a world where femininity is generally perceived to be inferior. Other boys, including siblings, will generally respond in the same way. "When my brother spoke to me about [being homosexual]," one respondent noted, "it was to tell me that I didn't have the right to live."

Young persons marginalized for reasons related to skin colour, religion, or a physical handicap can expect to find help and encouragement at home. The same, however, does not apply for young homosexual males. Once they risk revealing their homosexuality to family members, they will then discover whether support will or will not be forthcoming. In such a situation, family members will not only need to respond positively to the revelation but must also begin supporting the boy who is experiencing great injustices outside the family. Such supportive outcomes are alas uncommon. Ostracized homosexual adolescents do not get the sort of help made available to other youth marginalized for reasons related to ethnic origin, religious beliefs, handicap status, and so on. Neither do gay or bisexual adolescents generally benefit from the support of elders or mentors who have experienced similar problems; unfortunately, society generally frowns on youth being influenced by homosexual adults. Therefore, for many youth discovering their homosexuality, the isolation is often total. When they are subjected to one or more of the many forms of violence reserved for them, no one will protect them, assert their rights, or defend them.

This isolation is also predicated on two social reactions reported by most young gay men in our study. There is the shame-response incitation: *We must not speak about this, it must remain unknown.* Homosexuality is seen not as a positive attribute but as a fault of character. There is also the social stigmatization of visible homosexual desires and related behaviours and individuals. One respondent comments: "I was told that I was my family's shame, the neighbourhood's shame, and that this would drive my parents insane."

The inducement of shame begins early in a little boy's life, usually in association with learning that masculinity is superior to femininity, that being compared to a girl is intolerable, and that religion condemns homosexuality – did not the pope restate this on the occasion of the 2000 Jubilee and since? In addition, no parent would ever want to "have one" in the family. Being treated as a fag is the worst thing that could happen to a boy's status as a male.

In most adolescent environments in which respondents found themselves, homosexuality was not a legitimate topic of conversation, except when aspects of homosexuality were being ridiculed or dismissed, replicating common practice on many popular radio and television programs. One respondent remembers, "When my uncles came home to visit, they would always tell fag jokes." From these lessons, the young boy quickly learns that hiding his same-sex desires would best serve his interests. If he is identified as homosexual, he has been taught that he should not complain about any of the indignities inflicted upon him. The most he can expect is that his existence will be tolerated. As Erving Goffman (1964) notes, the stigmatized one must not give the impression through his visibility that he is even slightly abusing the tolerance granted to him, because great intolerance will quickly return. In the early years the Perfect Boys and the Chameleons seek to protect themselves from such judgments via invisibility, but their lives are dominated by great anxiety that they may be "discovered." Should this happen, they will certainly share the fate reserved for their more visible counterparts. The self-esteem of any boy could be destroyed by such an outcome.

For the young homosexual males who attempted suicide, shame and self-hatred were common emotions, along with the belief that they were unworthy of living. They had all been subjected to constant daily conditioning to convince them of their inferiority to other boys, and in particular the supposedly most masculine of them. Adding to their problems was the fact that positive gay role models – those living happy lives – were not really available. Even though some positive media portrayal of homosexual people is beginning, few successful gay individuals are willing to risk public revelation of their homosexuality. The youth in question also understand that without great wealth, power, or influence, it is better to walk in the shadows.

Even the Rebel who has succeeded somewhat in countering the effects of a closed and hostile environment often despairs at the magnitude of the awaiting task; this is his major vulnerability, in spite of his courage. Having to constantly fight alone to have his rights respected and to have others stop treating him as a deviant is a monumental task for a child or an adolescent.

The social stigmatization of homosexuality demonstrated by the abusive experiences that many respondents reported needs to be brought to public attention. From the time their homosexuality was recognized, these youths became objects of harassment, ridicule, and insults, including psychological, physical, and even sexual forms of violence. All of this they generally experienced in a climate indifferent to their torments. It would not be an exaggeration to compare the situation of young homosexual males – rejected or even physically assaulted by their fathers, made into scapegoats at school, and feeling hopelessly alone – to the plight of sexually abused boys (Dorais 2002). Youths marginalized because of their homosexuality, like boys who are sexually abused, must also suffer in silence and keep secret what they are made to endure; they begin to see potential aggressors in everyone, young or adult. The social abuses experienced by many of our respondents should have resulted in interventions with both the victims and their harassers. While in recent years important campaigns have led to more knowledge about victims of sexual abuse and improvements in our compassion and support, a similar education is still far away with respect to young homosexual males or gender-nonconformable boys.

Facing apparently insurmountable problems, combined with the more or less negative environmental responses to their existence (the best possible outcome experienced by some respondents was indifference), youths are likely to lose all joy in life or even the wish to live. Many professionals tend to associate depression with young men who attempt suicide, but for our respondents their condition is more likely exhaustion and hopelessness, which have little to do with psychological or mental dysfunction. Their situations can objectively be linked to outcomes such as wanting to end their lives; the abuses have become a burden too heavy to bear. Often complicating the situation are other problems such as grief over a death, the aftermath to child sexual abuse, the overuse of drugs, or relationship break-ups. Says Jean-François of his decision to end his life, "For a year I had been suffering from all the pressures – my father, my family … When I experienced total academic failure, I told myself, It's enough! It's not worth suffering to that point!"

Often, as in Nicholas's case, referred to in the preface of this study, the triggering event comes at the end of a long period of suffering in silence: being identified as homosexual, or fearing to be so identified, in a society in which no room has been made for gay youth. Gay adults, as a result of persistent efforts, have gained certain rights and liberties, even though this work is far from ended. But numerous homosexual youth problems remain unrecognized and unaddressed. Far too many people are still scandalized at the idea of granting to youth discovering their homosexual desires the same liberties and hopes accorded to heterosexual youth. Boys reporting their heterosexual desires are generally greeted with the affirmation that they have "become a man," as they were encouraged to become, and no one thinks that proselytizing has occurred. The opposite, however, applies with respect to same-sex desires. The current ideology seems to be that before eighteen years of age, homosexual individuals do not exist – or at least should not exist. Youths who become suicidal because of this injunction are most obviously victims of widespread discrimination and intolerance.

7

Resiliency Factors

Not all young men discovering their homosexual orientation want to kill themselves. In an effort to advance our understanding of why some individuals manage to cope with apparently similar life situations without crises, we interviewed young gay men who had never considered suicide. When their situations were compared to those of young men who had attempted suicide, two differences became apparent. Firstly, the degree of isolation, the inducement to feel shame, and the amount of ostracism experienced all play a role in the coping behaviours of young homosexual males. Those who sought to end their lives had become more psychologically exhausted, to the point of no return, when facing the stigma and abuses related to their homosexual orientation.

Secondly, there are a number of "protective" factors that appear to be helpful as some boys recognize their homosexual orientation and begin to face the associated difficulties, including their feelings of isolation, shame, and ostracism. These factors are also known as "resilience." Boris Cyrulnik (1999: 10) elaborates on this concept in his book *Un merveilleux malheur* (*A Wonderful Misfortune*): "When the word 'resilience' was conceived in physics, it described the ability of a body to resist shock … When the word was adapted in the social sciences, it was used to describe the capacity to live and develop positively, as socially defined, in spite of the kind of stress or adversity that would normally result in a very high risk for a negative outcome." Resiliency at its best is the capacity to come out of situational, temporary, and/or existential crises not weakened but with renewed strength. Thus distress does not necessarily lead to negative outcomes, including fatal ones.

It seems that even if young gay men suffer from injustice, discrimination, and ostracism in our society, a number of them profit from attributes that help them survive in hostile environments. Mario, a young man who did not become suicidal, reports of his former life situation, "The more I was mistreated by my father, the more I was harassed by my uncle, the more the guys treated me as a fag, the more I was convinced that they were assholes and that I was the one who was okay." Even though this young man's recognition of his homosexuality is perceived to be a burden (and the majority of related messages from the family, schools, and the media are of this nature), he is able to view his homosexual "difference" positively. Although few messages are available to help a youth perceive his homosexuality as something enviable, some individuals such as Mario do accomplish this feat. "I believed that all guys were homosexual: that this attribute was hiding at least somewhere in them," he says. "I could not get to believe that guys could have desires for females, only for females. I would tell myself that they were all a bunch of liars. I, at least, was the honest one."

Some factors are therefore helpful to homosexual youth, given that adversity must be confronted and that negative outcomes are to be minimized. For example, these factors can include:

- a healthy determination to criticize and contradict the opinions of others ("They will not get to me – I will succeed in spite of them!"), a certain independence of thought ("I have the right to be different, to not be like everyone else");

- a sense of humour when facing adversity (camp humour, an ironic mixture of exaggeration and mockery, being a good example), a creativity that permits one to dream as a way of compensating for reality (for example, as in the film *Ma vie en rose*, where the young Ludovic – rejected by all because of his femininity and his possible homosexuality or transsexuality – escapes in his dreams);

- well-established significant relationships (a father, mother, grandparent, brother, sister, friend, a teacher on whom one can depend unconditionally);

- the awareness or even the celebration of one's potential in spite of degradation by others ("I knew I was intelligent, that I had talents").

Some young stigmatized males exposed to various forms of violence and psychological abuse, including traumatic experiences, may refuse to remain passive in such situations (even more than Rebels do) (Dorais, 2002). They may also become fighters for their rights and liberties. Some interviewed homosexual youth had begun to work with groups formed to help others. "I wanted to help others avoid what I had gone through," says Johnny, a member of such a group; he had recently made a presentation in the same school he had dropped out of two years before because of the ostracism he was subjected to. Jean-Paul was proactive while still in school: "I founded the gay organization in my high school, and it still exists, although no one now knows that I founded it. My name will not end up in history books, but I did mark history with my desire to help others, even if this resulted in some small problems for me." The altruism manifested in these two stories is a positive attribute that gives these young men even more reason to fight on, and to want to live.

Interestingly, some youths previously exposed to problems such as divorce of their parents or the death of a love one, and who have had the experience of resolution of these problems well before their homosexuality came to the forefront, sometimes appear to be better equipped to cope with the new crisis. That is, such experiences may help them to tackle other problems, including serious ones. On the other hand, children or adolescents who have always been protected from problems may experience their recognized homosexuality as an insurmountable difficulty. The same may apply to the recognition of anticipated problems in their lives and the need to confront and resolve them.

Given that the interpretation of what happens to us is at least as important as the facts themselves, it is likely that youths who refuse to interpret their homosexuality negatively do preserve their self-esteem, even in times of great adversity. They are also more combative. This is why, for example, so few Rebels were identified as suicidal in our study. They are far less likely to seek to end their lives because of their homosexuality. They accept themselves. Most important, however, is their refusal to internalize the environmental homophobia that has characterized our society and a great number of its institutions.

Many young gay men drop out of school because they respond adversely to a world that ignores or rejects them and also fails to protect them. Others, however, somehow persevere, telling themselves that their ultimate vengeance will be their academic success (such as obtaining a university degree) and/or their social successes (such as having a good career, doing well in the business world, having money). A youth who internalizes society's heterosexism and homophobia (which occurs, alas, in numerous cases) will likely degrade and hate himself, thus minimizing his perceived potential, sometimes to the point of believing that he does not deserve to live. On the other hand, the youth who is inclined to challenge the established order and related beliefs may find the motivation to fight when faced with discrimination and related injustices.

It must also be noted that young people, especially homosexual youths, generally have a strong need for affiliation, and that may include being part of a group where solidarity may be experienced. As Howard Becker (1963) emphasized for marginalized individuals, their belonging to a group often results in a renaissance that serves to counter their social rejection. Homosexual youths often feel that their homosexuality or gender nonconformity implies rejection from the groups they once belonged to (such as a village, neighbourhood, family, or peer group), and this loss of important social links may result in also losing the wish to live. To flourish, human beings must perceive themselves to be part of a whole greater than self. Therefore, when young gay or bisexual men feel rejected by certain groups, they must then recognize themselves to be part of a greater reality. Thus it may be helpful for them to learn that homosexuality has always existed in all cultures at all times, no matter what the inflicted abuses have been (Boswell 1980, 1994; Spencer 1995).

Although homosexuality in our culture has long been synonymous with sin, the unnatural, criminality, pathology, and related marginalization, homosexual desires are nonetheless present in a significant proportion of the population. In some areas, especially in larger cities, many of these individuals have decided to come together to (among other things) counter discrimination and experience solidarity. This applies, for example, to Montreal's Gay Village and, on a smaller scale, to many gay associations with varying interests such as discussion, sports, politics, education, and activism, and to meeting places where homosexual people are welcome, such as restaurants, bars, and coffee houses.

For some of our respondents, and also for others who did not experience suicide problems, the knowledge that certain safe places existed where they would be able to meet others like themselves gave them courage and hope. This happened even before they were old enough to venture into these places. The existence of gay youth groups such as Project 10, Lambda Youth, or organized discussion or helping groups in some community centres is crucial, given that they fill a major gap in social services. Very few gay youths are able to socialize spontaneously in their native environments, given that "the closet" is imposed on them and that other homosexual youths generally remain invisible. Therefore, not only is this sharing of experiences (problems as well as solutions) highly recommended to end the isolation and dead-end situations for homosexual youths, but these youths, like all young people, need to develop and experience both casual and significant friendships as well as love relationships. Most important, however, is their association with a peer group and the resulting feeling of belonging to the group.

Stigmatized youths meeting others with similar experiences often produce feelings of great solidarity, as Howard Becker (1963) emphasizes. The affiliation with a peer group is a significant step in identity construction for marginalized individuals, and this source of solidarity has many benefits, including learning from peers about how to live with a marginalized status as comfortably as possible. Socializing with peers, in summation, will help to overcome isolation and gradually reduce the shame resulting from being "different," as well as provide support, mutual help, and the encouragement necessary to confront ostracism and intolerance. As Émile Durkheim asserts, integration into a community, no matter what the community may be, reduces the individual risk of suicide.

8

Recommendations for Suicide Prevention

All efforts towards the prevention of suicide must identify the risk factors to be tackled and eliminated or at least minimized. Resilience or protective factors must also be identified, with the objective of creating them or, if they are already in existence, making them more effective. Although significant advances have recently been made with respect to suicide, it seems that self-identified young gay males and males identified (correctly or incorrectly) by others as homosexual have been neglected in prevention efforts. Helping these young men will require specific measures, often unique to them, and the expansion of general precepts to be more inclusive of this social subgroup.

The following interrelated recommendations are described along three axes, summarized as follows:

1 Ending the isolation of these young men by extending a hand and also making feelings of solidarity possible.
2 Ending their feelings of shame by extending full equality and social acceptance to them.
3 Countering stigmatization by implanting full respect for human diversity.

Schools are a pivotal element of the socialization process, and they should be privileged places of learning about respect of self and others. The opposite often applies, however, for homosexual or "feminine" boys who are marginalized in schools. This is related to the freedom that boys have traditionally had to be as homophobic as possible (Plummer 1999). Furthermore, through what is said or not said about sexuality in general and homosexuality in particular, school personnel all too often perpetuate the ignorance that breeds hopelessness and anguish in individuals on one hand, and taboos and prejudices in their social environments on the other. Teachers and administrators frequently turn a blind eye to the sexist and homophobic statements and behaviour of students and school staffs, thus contributing to the abuse and exclusion problems of boys self-identified as homosexual or identified as such by others. As a result, many of our respondents had dropped out of school, temporarily or permanently, because they "could not take it anymore."

How many youths with a homosexual orientation are there in schools? Only one study in Quebec, carried out by GRIS (Groupe de recherches et d'information sociale) Chaudière-Appalache,[*] has attempted to do such an estimate based on sexual activity and sexual desires. The research was carried out between October 1998 and June 2000. The results from more than 3,300 questionnaires distributed in classrooms to secondary students in levels 3, 4, and 5, and at the college level indicated that about 10 per cent of students between fourteen and nineteen had had "an experience or a sexual relationship with an individual of the same sex." Almost 5 per cent were wholly or partly sexually attracted to same-sex individuals, and 1.5 per cent replied to the sexual attraction question with "I do not

---

[*] The cited data were supplied to us by GRIS Chaudière-Appalaches.

know." The number of youth who are conscious of their homosexuality or bisexuality is thus not insignificant, and the results would likely have been higher if the students answering the questionnaire had been assured of a greater degree of confidentiality. Nonetheless, the results are similar to ones from studies of large samples of North American adults.**

It is odd but perhaps symptomatic that while school systems have increasingly taken on the task of reflecting aspects of social diversity such as ethnic and cultural diversity, they have remained mostly resistant to advocacy for sexual diversity. Furthermore, at a time when young homosexual individuals suffer from a cruel lack of "positive role models," few gay or bisexual teachers have made their homosexual orientation publicly known. Possibly such information is relegated to the private sphere. Yet their heterosexual counterparts rarely hesitate to reveal that they have an opposite-sex partner, or children, or even that they spent a weekend with an opposite-sex partner. Two value systems exist here, reflecting the fact that homosexuality and bisexuality continue to be perceived as something more or less shameful and to be hidden. They are seen as "bad examples" to give youth.

This being said, in Quebec the new "Program of Programs" for primary schools (MEQ 2000) launched in September 2000 could become a venue for change if gender and sexual-diversity issues were implemented. For example, among the "domains of life experiences" proposed to teachers and children, in at least four out of eight dimensions, activities related to the respect of

---

** On this subject, see Kinsey et al. (1948), *Sexual Behavior;* Hite (1983), *The Hite Report on Male Sexuality;* Janus and Janus (1993), *The Janus Report on Sexual Behavior;* Laumann et al. (1994), *The Social Organization of Sexuality.*

self and others in association with gender and love/sex attraction differences could easily be included. This addition would be important given that the document notes, in reference to health and well-being, that "students will acquire a thoughtful disposition with respect to developing healthy behaviours associated with their health, well-being, sexuality and security." Further, in the section dealing with "personal, academic, and professional orientation," the student is to "undertake and complete projects related to self-realization and social integration." The ongoing encouragement of the student's socio-relational development is emphasized and, finally, he/she is also to learn about life in society "with an open mind about people and with a respect for diversity and differences." The document accents the highly valued skill known as "the ability to solve problems," this being one of Cyrulnik's resiliency factors, as we have seen.

If these objectives turn out to be more than words or wishes, and if a few items are added such as the masculinity/femininity spectrum (gender issues), heterosexuality, homosexuality, and bisexuality (sexual and emotional orientations), then long-overdue sexual diversity issues would begin to be addressed. In addition, because the program speaks directly about "a vision of the world enriched through encounters with difference and diversity," it would be important to not exclude certain differences such as gender and sexual/emotional attraction. In the present program, however, silence rules with respect to these realities and other traditionally taboo subjects such as intersexuality and transgender/multi-gender issues.

Alas, the present school program does not encourage the systematic use of inclusive language. It is important for children to be aware that a boy or girl, or a man or a woman, could have a same-sex boyfriend or girlfriend. The possibility that parents may be of the same or different sexes (or may be intersexual, transsexual, or transgender) is also a subject of interest, but generally is passed over silence. Why? Using inclusive language would be a reasonable way of recognizing these realities, thereby making a little room in discourses for those individuals who are different. In fact, it is often through the inclusion or exclusion of such details that a youth will learn about what is or is not acceptable. This is why the frequent silences in schools surrounding homosexuality and gender issues cannot be viewed as neutral. To not talk about something or to avoid certain subjects indicates that these realities apparently do not deserve to be addressed. As well, school materials such as texts and workbooks have incorporated little or nothing on sexual and gender diversity issues.

While our study was in progress, we heard the principal of one school justify on the basis of real or anticipated objections being raised by parents his inaction with respect to supplying information about sexual diversity and fighting homophobia. Would a similar response apply if racist parents, as adherents to white supremacist ideologies, demanded that children of colour not be treated with equality? Would the desires of parents wanting the Sharia law to be applied in incidences of theft also be adhered to? Would the principal accept that a youth's hand be cut off in such cases? The answer is no, but not because parents do not have the right to their beliefs and related values. Schools must advocate for the equality and respect of human dignity and integrity. If the wishes and the values of certain individuals or groups are to be considered, they must not prevail if they are in violation of the values embodied in the laws and charters of Canadian society. As the writer Amin Maalouf has noted (1998: 142), "respecting traditions or laws that discriminate against others is equivalent to hating the victims." That is, if some parents motivated by hatred would rather see their child dead than homosexual, we cannot collectively endorse this judgment and behave accordingly. Given these facts and other realities addressed in this book, schools must therefore begin to speak about homosexuality, homophobia, and gender-related issues in unbiased and inclusive ways. This will help young people in non-normative categories to better understand their situation, and it will also help their peers develop tolerance, respect, and even a desperately needed understanding of human diversity.

We must recognize as well that youths speaking or acting in homophobic ways require intervention, in much the same way that interventions occur with respect to racism and other forms of intolerance based on ethnic and religious differences. Studies show that it is boys – or groups of boys – who most often commit homophobic acts and crimes. They have great difficulty expressing their masculinity in positive ways and manifest intolerance for everything that seems strange or different to them. These boys are also excellent candidates for delinquency, vandalism, and many forms of violence (Appleby and Anastas, 1998). It is most unwise to ignore or minimize their behaviours, and the same applies to their problems. School personnel, social services, child and youth protection agencies, and the police should intervene as quickly as possible in these situations. Their prime objective would be prevention so that the situation does not worsen, with remedial education being a major focus.

Boys correctly or incorrectly identified as homosexual as well as "feminine" boys need to be in safe schools where they will be respected and protected from prejudice-related harassment and violence – children's rights include having such safe environments. The learning of hatred for others (homophobia) and self-hatred (internalized homophobia) should have no place in schools. Unfortunately, many of the study subjects reported being forced to end their studies in secondary schools (or at least having had to change schools) to escape the hatred and violence they were experiencing. Homosexual boys are at high risk for dropping out of school. Given our awareness of the elevated school dropout rate for boys in Quebec in particular, it would be unwise to ignore the possible homophobic aspects of this problem.

At this point it may be of value to consider the increasing success of girls in schools. It has been suggested that such positive results stem in great part from girls being encouraged to use their full human potential: their masculine and feminine attributes. Boys, on the other hand, continue to be raised with a great fear that anyone might "suspect" them to be feminine, "like a girl." This is especially so because feminine attributes in males are usually equated with homosexuality, and related sanctions continue to be severe for all boys violating what is deemed to be "masculine." While the quest for the equality of the sexes is advancing, the quest for gender equality (masculinity and femininity being of equal value) remains to be tackled in schools and elsewhere. Most troubling, however, is not the fact that many boys consider academic success to be feminine, as they are sometimes heard to say, but that the "feminine" epithets directed at any male are sufficient to totally discredit him.

With the help of feminism, schools have made great strides in giving girls access to traditional male domains. But everything remains to be done with respect to gender equality – masculinity and femininity – as human characteristics or qualities, independent of the individual's sex or sexual orientation. More should be done in general and extracurricular school activities to have situations where "the feminine" is given as much value as "the masculine," with the understanding that both attributes are part of every individual, each also having associations with sexual diversity. Without doubt, such an education would greatly benefit all students. The proposed education should be focused on the elimination of homophobia and effeminophobia that are intimately related to the hatred and stigmatization of feminine attributes in males. Accomplishing this, however, will require more than fully recognizing the equality of genders in addition to the equality of the sexes. Children will need to be taught to have pride in both their differences and similarities to others. Pride in itself is not only the opposite of shame: it is the remedy for the problem and its antidote.

In Quebec as in many other societies, males have a history of being thought of as "unmanly" if they have manifested any interest in culture. This was illustrated by a government minister during the Duplessis years (the 1940s and 1950s) who bragged of never having opened a book in his life! In this respect, society has a long way to go. As long as boys who succeed better academically than in sports are believed to be "faggy," the problem will remain. Hockey players, especially the most violent of them, continue to be idealized. Male figure skaters and ballet dancers are often ridiculed; the stereotype is that such men are less than male, or "feminine," usually meaning "homosexual." These realities indicate that sexism, effeminophobia, and homophobia remain as salient attributes of our society.

If schools are serious about the wish to venture into the respect of differences and diversity, as we are led to believe from the newly espoused philosophies, the education of school personnel is most important. As a rule, they have not received sufficient education with respect to sex/love attractions and gender diversity, mostly because these subjects have been generally absent from the teacher education curricula in colleges and universities. In particular, physical education teachers should be concerned about these issues because, according to our respondents, some of the most hurtful and harmful manifestations of sexism, effeminophobia, and homophobia occurred in physical-education classes or related activities such as undressing in locker rooms and taking showers.

In the past few years the Quebec Ministry of Health and Social Services created a three-part sensitization program on homosexuality through the Centre Québécois de Coordination sur le Sida (Quebec Coordination Center for AIDS). This program was given with great success to health and social services professionals and also, upon request, to those specializing in helping youth, including teachers. The sensitization sessions are called "For a New Vision of Homosexuality: Intervening to Increase Respect for Sexual Orientations Diversity" and "Adapting Our Interventions to Homosexual Realities (Part 1: The Young, Their Families, and Their Life Environments," and "Part 2: Adults, Couples, and Their Relatives").*** These intense one-day education sessions make it possible to lessen the impact of traditional ignorance in the helping professions by increasing knowledge about homosexuality and the discomfort commonly felt when addressing these issues.

Adapting and widely distributing such educational material (especially the section on youth) to school personnel is highly recommended, given our study results. The testimonies of many study subjects indict school personnel in the reported abuses, and it must be conceded that the absence of philosophical and pedagogical support with respect to gender and sexual diversity has fostered such indifference. At its worst, the

---

***The French titles of these documents are: "Pour une nouvelle vision de l'homosexualité: intervenir dans le respect de la diversité des orientations sexuelles" and "Adapter nos interventions aux réalités homosexuelles" ("Volet 1: Les jeunes, leurs familles et leurs milieux de vie" et "Volet 2: Les adultes, leurs couples et leurs proches").

existing situation has supported – in a conscious or unconscious manner – ideologies that underlie the various abuses reported by many respondents.

It is difficult to explain why sexual diversity issues have received so little attention in the training of those entering the teaching professions and in the continuing education of professionals. At best, the taboo status of any sexuality deemed to be non-reproductive must be invoked, meaning that all sexualities lying outside the heterosexual norm are apparently unacceptable. This situation exists as much for teachers as it does for those in other helping professions such as social workers, psychologists, and police – that is, for all who intervene with individuals manifesting a plurality of values, customs, and sexual/emotional preferences. This shortcoming is costly to society because it also contributes to the perpetuation of existing problems and the generating of others, as opposed to resolving problems. Ignorance, indifference, and silence, whether we are conscious of them or not, are often the greatest allies of intolerance (see also Lipkin 2000).

In spite of the women's movement and its male allies, masculinity continues to be perceived as superior to femininity. For a girl, it is not a bad thing to be somewhat masculine. In fact, who has not heard a father celebrating the sporting exploits of his daughter, sometimes approvingly deemed to be "a real tomboy"? The reverse of this situation, however, does not apply. A boy manifesting feminine attributes is said to be "effeminate," with highly negative implications. These boys are never their fathers' pride and joy, and they only rarely have their mothers' approval. It is not surprising that the earlier-identified males in our study (those identified as homosexual very early in their lives, usually as a result of their detectable femininity) all reported experiencing difficult relationships with their fathers and often with their mothers as well.

When faced with the discovery or revelation that a son is homosexual, the family (parents and siblings) are often traumatized and distressed. At best, they do not know how to respond, at least at the beginning. Homosexuality is not part of the human possibilities presented to parents, or to children. Thus families often need counselling and support to help them deal with their uncertainties, prejudices, fears, and questions. The help of professionals, or lay people such as parents with similar experiences who have formed small support helping groups, has been precious. This kind of help should be made available in community centres, at centres for the protection of children and youth, and at schools. Ideally, related community initiatives should also be occurring throughout North America, so that all families, including those in rural areas, have access to such services when needed.

We also believe that it is the responsibility of government agencies for the protection of youth and for human rights to intervene in cases where an individual's integrity and rights (as granted, for example, in Quebec's Charter of Rights and Liberties) are not being respected. This especially applies in situations of family and school violence involving children and youth apparently not conforming to the gender or sexual orientation expectations of others. Such violence endangers the health and security of these individuals and should therefore be forbidden, with the emphasis being on educating those who violate the rights of others. The fact that many youths in our study had to drop out of school to avoid homophobic violence is very troubling. It is tragic that these young people often ended up alone and sometimes suicidal, and that they were unable to obtain help. For some, the streets became home, where they practised prostitution for survival. There were few other places where these boys would have been welcomed and where some of their more basic needs for food and shelter could have been met. These outcomes are completely unacceptable whether a youth is homosexual, heterosexual, or gender nonconformable.

Basically, all youth should have access to community resources such as counselling, special referrals if needed, and shelter when, among many reasons including sexual orientation or gender nonconformity, they are rejected by their families and life has been made impossible for them in school. With respect to the ostracism gay youth experience or fear, resources specifically directed at their needs should be identified, published, and made widely available. Rejected youth will know then that they have options. They may access safe resources where, in addition to being welcome and understood, they may find someone to advocate for them and perhaps also mediate in problems with family or school.

The facts presented in the section of our study dealing with public places and related dangers should be used to sensitize the police about the importance of acting in preventative and protective ways and, as needed, intervening in cases involving homophobic intimidation, threats, and violence. The Quebec school for the training of police devotes a part of a course to gay and lesbian issues, but the teaching of related issues should be more than minimal. Quebec's provincial police force has also implemented a program for youth problem prevention in its ongoing education program for police officers. It is called "Cool pour vrai – Désamorcer des conflits, prévenir des crimes" (Really Cool: Diffusing Conflicts and Crime Prevention) and could be used in many interesting ways within the context of the socially created problems outlined in this book.

Services directed at youth should be made highly sensitive to the fate often inflicted on gay young men and others abused in similar ways because they are believed to be homosexual.

This would include knowing about the varied forms of violence inflicted on these boys and their high risk for experiencing numerous problems, with the potential for suicide. In addition, regional and national resources should be equipped to provide specialized services to these youths. Two study respondents reported that the discovery of a resource such as Gai Écoute/Gay Line had been so beneficial that it had essentially prevented renewed attempts at killing themselves. While all intervening individuals should be able to listen attentively and help these young men, these youths often benefit even more from talking with one of their "own kind" – sometimes the first time that such an event occurs. For these reasons, services like Gai Écoute/Gay Line that operate on a twenty-four hour basis are essential, given that crises may be experienced at any time. The availability of such services should be widely publicized in all areas where youth gather, including schools.

Because the homosexual or bisexual orientation of adults in society remains generally hidden, gay youth are denied access to elders who have experienced similar difficulties and overcome them. It is known, however, that the relating of such experiences to distressed young people can be of great value. For one respondent, meeting an openly gay teacher supplied him with a positive role model that permitted him to recognize the astonishing possibility of being gay, respected, and respectable. One could be both gay and happy! The education projects and conferences made possible by some youth groups (such as Safe Places, Project 10, and Lambda Youth), and by some community groups such as Gai Écoute/Gay Line have also been of great value. Schools and resources for youth have especially benefited from these educational activities, meaning that their quality and frequency should also be increased, with funds being made available to support them.

Countering the traditional silence and invisibility with respect to sexual and gender diversity issues will require specific effort, hard work, and more funding. It must be emphasized that the issue is not one of encouraging or discouraging a particular sexual preference through the dissemination of information, as some critics may assert. It is a matter of recognizing and respecting sexual and gender diversity (Dorais 1999) and eliminating intolerance. The objective is to challenge erroneous beliefs and related prejudices that have unfortunately contributed to making the lives of many young men impossible, to the point that they consider suicide and perhaps carry it out.

In brief, homosexually oriented youths do not require special treatment, but they do deserve, like everyone else, recognition of their potential and their problems. They also deserve respect, empathy, comprehension, and moral support when required. To make sure that they benefit from the goodwill that all young people ought to be granted, a few policies must be in place. Helping professionals in social services must be sensitized to the realties of these youths, and those designated to address related issues must be adequately educated and supported. This is of monumental importance because almost everything remains to be done to improve the fate of this group, to reduce their high rates for attempting suicide and thereby to save lives. A broad campaign to sensitize the public is essential, with special focus placed on school personnel, the police, and those in youth-related social services. These professionals must be encouraged to expand existing services, requiring at times the development and use of resources specifically related to homosexually oriented and gender nonconformable youths. All must also work to improve the social climate by encouraging acceptance of sexual and gender diversity.

This leads us to briefly address the role of the media in propagating and perpetuating biases and prejudices. The media also has the potential for promoting a culture more accepting of sexual and gender diversity. Government agencies that often partly or wholly support the production of films, television series, and documentaries and that regulate the use of the airways should become more active regarding social intolerance issues. All too often, gay people are marginalized and made ridiculous in the media. Our charters of human rights specify that we should have basic respect for others, but this has not been the case on many television and radio programs. Programs have been aired that degraded homosexual people – often under the guise of humour – to the point of sometimes inciting hatred for this group.

The intent is not to forbid humour related to homosexuality, given that humour in all facets of life does have value. The problem has been that, with respect to homosexuality, humour is all that was being heard, with very few other discourses receiving attention, particularly during peak viewing and listening hours. The existence of intolerant "religious" discourse on air is shocking: freedom of religion should not mean freedom to hate. These restricted discourses serve to support and even reinforce sexism, effeminophobia, and homophobia. Directly or indirectly, violence has been one result of this situation, both towards designated "others" (in this case called "homophobic violence") and towards the self. A young gay male may terminate his life because his socially learned self-hatred happens to be as intense as the hatred manifested by other males who seek out homosexual people to assault and even murder them. Given these facts, would it not be a positive development if the media began making some efforts to help youth be more accepting of sexual diversity? Surely the presentation in the media of more positive and realistic homosexual, bisexual, and gender role models is long overdue. The past few years have seen some improvement, but there is still much to be done.

It has been said that suicide is a final solution to a temporary problem. Unfortunately, young homosexual males are often set up to see nothing positive in their future. This situation is greatly exacerbated by the non-recognition of their realities, including their general rejection by all concerned. This situation contributes greatly to their suicidal feelings and related suicide attempts. All too often these young people have lost faith in human nature. Their suicide attempts, completed or not, reflect the punishment they are inflicting on themselves, the result of the socially induced self-hatred and shame they have been made to feel simply because they were "not like the others."

Homosexual and bisexual male youth suicide problems are the direct and predictable consequence of our society not having made any space for these youths. Most of or maybe even all of us have somehow conspired to produce the same message: we would prefer that they not exist. Some of these young men have behaved accordingly. They are now dead. Sadly, even after death, they remain stigmatized, not only because they were homosexual but also because they committed suicide. In cases where no one suspected the youth of being homosexual, we may have heard people say, "Why would such a wonderful boy have committed suicide when he had so much to live for?" In this study, we have supplied at least one possible answer to the question.

9

Challenging Homophobia
to Prevent Suicide:
Mission Possible

The responses to the first publication of this study at the end of 2000 surpassed all expectations. There were hundreds of media interviews and invitations to speak in schools and to community groups and diverse organizations in French Canada and Europe. Presentations were made at local, national, and international gatherings and conferences. We were astonished at the general public's acceptance of the topic of young gay men who have attempted suicide. Yet not all the responses were positive.

Some suicidologists have vehemently resisted the proposed link between homophobia (internalized by homosexually oriented youth or manifested by their environment) and suicidality among boys targeted for harassment because they are seen as homosexual. For example, a highly placed individual involved with suicide prevention in France, commenting on North American quantitative and qualitative research related to this issue, was quoted in *Le Monde* as saying: "I am not convinced of the quality of these studies." One of his colleagues angrily added, "Why then not be concerned about those small in stature, the overweight ones, and disfigured youth?" For these experts in suicidology, the life experiences of young gay males, or those identified as such, do not warrant research investigation to better understand why they attempt or commit suicide. Even greater vehemence was exhibited by a school principal responding to a student who wanted these issues to be discussed in school: "I work for the 90 per cent of students who are normal [meaning: heterosexual], NOT for the others." Obviously the resistance can be enormous. Without doubt, some professionals would rather see these youths dead as opposed to ever seeking to understand and help them.

Homophobia, especially in its predictable results such as slurs and abuses of all kinds directed at young gay, lesbian, and bisexual individuals, is producing highly negative outcomes. This is especially evident in schools, as reported in our study. Blatant as well as more covert incitements to anti-gay violence and socially induced internalized homophobia will continue to ruin lives for as long as there is no firm commitment in place to have these issues addressed. Accomplishing this end, however, will require the active participation of political organizations, schools, student associations, and parents, as well as all who are concerned about human suffering stemming from intolerance, including intolerance against sexual diversity.

In spite of the historical negativity vis-à-vis homosexuality in North America, gay, lesbian, and bisexual people are not condemned to being lifelong victims. Far from it, and this fact is to be emphasized. Our recent history reveals that homosexually oriented people can be motivated to challenge discriminatory laws and social practices. Although full equality between heterosexually and homosexually oriented people is a long process and not yet a *fait accompli*, recent positive changes that have occurred are cause for optimism. For example, same-sex unions have increasingly been recognized in Canada, along with parenting and adoption rights. But these improvements have been the result of intense lobbying. Vigilance must be maintained, given that our society may return to a past status quo where members of sexual diversity groups are treated as inferior. Demagogues remain ready as always to target with their specious reasoning anyone "different" and thus deemed to be "dangerous." Fortunately, the anti-homosexuality elements in society do not have a monopoly on free speech nor the near absolute power they would need to implement their desires.

We would like to describe here some recent positive changes that have occurred in Quebec, noting that the past fifty years have been marked by "the quiet revolution," as Quebec society has increasingly turned away from its ultra-Catholic and highly conservative past. Quebec is now manifesting an open spirit, even with respect to homosexuality. By 1977 it became the second society in the world to include "sexual orientation" within the categories protected from discrimination in its charter of rights. Fifteen years later, the Quebec government became the first in the world to establish a commission of public inquiry to report on discrimination and violence experienced by homosexually oriented people. The commission's 1993 report to the Quebec National Assembly made forty-one recommendations. These focused on reducing homophobia and on making possible the full equality in society of homosexually oriented people. By 1999 laws were being changed so that same-sex partners had equal rights with heterosexual partners, and by 2002 full equality was granted with respect to parental and adoption rights. These advances, however, did not happen by accident. They were the result of constant pressure and the organized efforts of many gay and lesbian groups and their supporters, including more progressive feminists groups who rallied to form a common front when required.

Other developments also helped to positively change perspectives on homosexuality. At the beginning of the AIDS epidemic in North America, Quebec's public health authorities recognized that the groups most affected by the disease were generally unknown to health professionals and those working in social services. As a result, a working group predominantly composed of gay professionals and an advisory committee representing Quebec's major gay and lesbian groups was formed in 1991 with a mandate to develop a sensitization workshop for health and social services professionals. By 1993 the program "Pour une nouvelle vision de l'homosexualité: Intervenir dans le respect de la diversité des orientations sexuelles" (For a New Vision of Homosexuality: Intervening to Increase Respect for Sexual Orientation Diversity) was ready to be piloted and evaluated by a group of independent researchers. The objective was to make it a permanent program subject to ongoing evaluations and improvements. The day-long workshop was offered at no cost to any group of twenty professionals requesting it, wherever they were located in the province of Quebec. The largest numbers of requests came from medical doctors, nurses, social workers, psychologists, educators, volunteer workers, suppliers of home care services, and administrators involved in providing services and hiring personnel. Over the years the program has been expanded and adapted to meet the needs of other professionals such as police officers, teachers of all grades in public schools, other school personnel, and those working in the area of human rights.

By 2003, over ten thousand people had participated in these education sessions, far exceeding initial estimates. The program is now one of the more popular offered by Quebec's Ministry of Health and Social Services. This outcome was likely the result of many professionals recognizing that their education on homosexuality issues had been lacking, even non-existent. In fact, until very recently, not one of Quebec's universities or other educational institutions offered a course on homosexuality that would have been helpful to professionals in health fields and social services.

As the result of requests from many who attended the program, two additional programs have been developed since 1997, as noted in the previous chapter. Their objectives have moved beyond sensitization to being more like required continuing professional education. The two programs have a common name: "Adapter nos interventions aux réalités homosexuelles" (Adapting Our Interventions to Homosexual Realities), with one section devoted to youth, their families, and their life environments, and the second section devoted to gay and lesbian adults, couples, and their relatives. A few thousand professionals have now participated in these continuing education programs given by the same teams of two professionals, preferably one lesbian and one gay male, some of whom are parents. This leadership has had positive results, especially when personal experiences are useful in supporting the educational content of these sessions. All the programs are organized under the direction of the Centre de coordination sur le sida (Quebec Coordination Center for AIDS, part of the Department of Health and Social Services), the regional divisions of Public Health, and a professional college. The in-service courses are recognized for continuing education credits.

The accumulating wealth of information acquired by the education teams and program director has increasingly caused many in the Department of Health and Social Services to recognize the need to integrate this education in all sectors. By 1997 the minister of Health and Social Services made known his wishes in *L'adaptation des services sociaux et de santé aux réalités homosexuelles (Adapting Health and Social Services to Homosexual Realities)*. This document legitimizes what was happening before and has happened since the education programs related to homosexuality were begun, the principles being:

- the elimination of all discrimination in health and social services;
- the recognition that aspiring to a better life by gay, lesbian, and bisexual people is warranted;
- the promotion of respect for all gay, lesbian, and bisexual people, including respect for differences.

These objectives are now being reflected in social services adapted to client realities and needs, in the assistance supplied to community groups and support services, and in the increasing development of knowledge and research in this field.

Our study (published in French as *Mort ou Fif*), the basis of *Dead Boys Can't Dance*, was the first research project to be funded under these new principles. Reaction to its publication was electrifying, with great and wide-ranging interest from the media and the public. One result was that the labour union group representing most of Quebec's public school teachers, La Centrale des Syndicats du Québec, decided to include anti-homophobia education as an immediate objective. Within a year a sensitization/education video, *Silence svp (Silence Please)*, was produced for use with both teachers and students. This video was eventually accompanied by a "first aid kit" financed by Public Health and the Department of Relations with Citizens and for Immigration. The kit includes resources for youth and their parents as well as anyone intervening to help (for example, the guide *Démystifier l'homosexualité: Ça commence à l'école [Demystifying Homosexuality: It Begins in School]*). Further, the Montreal school district, the largest in Quebec, now has a working group concerned with the situation of gay and lesbian youth in schools.

As the above events were happening, a primary supporter of our research, Gai Écoute/Gay Line (the Gay Line phone line service dedicated to helping gay, lesbian, bisexual, and questioning individuals, along with their family and friends), managed to have Quebec's major television networks air a highly moving excerpt of an interview related to the coming out of a major star of Quebec television. In the thirty-second free message aired at the beginning of evening prime time, Daniel Pinard says:

For an adolescent, discovering that one is gay is a tragedy. Yet none of this is a choice, and this is what troubles these youth the most. I am gay and it's not because I chose it! So, I decided to say this to all youth: I am telling them that there are solutions, that we can live gay and be happy, and that we can also enjoy growing older, even if a myth says otherwise. In fact, when we are gay, the older we get, the better life becomes. At least, this is what I believe. And the more I am happy with myself, the more I realize that I have nothing to prove to others.

This message was heard in all homes in Quebec without negative repercussions; in fact, the opposite occurred. The message resulted in many compliments being directed towards Pinard, and much sympathy being expressed for the situation faced by young gays and lesbians.

Another interesting phenomenon has been the increasing development of support groups for gay, lesbian, bisexual, and questioning adolescents and young adults. The development of these groups should be widely encouraged. Often, however, for such groups to develop and prosper, support is needed from adults deemed to be credible in the public eye because there are still some parents and administrators who believe that even hearing someone talk about homosexuality can cause young people to become homosexual! These groups began in the early 1970s, after social workers at a youth protection agency became concerned about the desperation experienced by some gay and lesbian youth. Since then, the groups have become more numerous. They now also exist in some rural areas where they are meeting some of the needs of sexual-minority youth (the legal age for consensual sexual activities in Canada is fourteen years in some cases, eighteen years in others). Some of these groups are a part of social services, while others are autonomous. Most have added "social action" to their mandate, and some young people from these groups have been actively participating in sensitization sessions in settings such as schools and youth homes.

As has been the case for older homosexually oriented people, young people have been coming out of a very dark closet and organizing themselves into groups. They have also been demanding respect from adults and peers and in many other situations in their daily lives. By the summer of 2001 more than 100,000 pamphlets had been sent to all schools in Quebec, through collaborative efforts among diverse gay and lesbian youth groups and the Department of Relations with Citizens and for Immigration. In this pamphlet, the Gai Écoute/Gay Line message was: "Teachers, dads, moms, make it possible for me to be happy." Photos featured one gay boy and one lesbian girl, both using their real names, and testimony by other young people concerning their lives. This little publication has taken on the silence and ignorance associated with male and female homosexualities that have traditionally existed in school and families.

All of these developments reveal that gay, lesbian, and bisexual people and their supporters, when acting as a common front and with solidarity, can be successful in increasing society's respect for sexual diversity. This achievement has included having more accurate social representations of homosexuality and also having major legal changes enacted. Early on, people of diverse sexual orientations recognized that they had been victims of homophobia and heterosexism, and this recognition was required for them to better understand how to end their victimization status. The process meant becoming actively involved in the improvement of our collective lives and in also advocating the equality of all in both private and public lives. This objective, representing the ideal for the future, is now within sight, but its realization still depends on our personal and professional dedication, and possibly some militant action. Above all, it depends upon our acting in solidarity.

We have to give to all young people the will to live and, if necessary, the will and the help to fight for their rights and liberties. We don't have to be gay or lesbian to believe in a better society, open to all the human diversity. A secure, caring, and loving environment is a good antidote for suicide among all youth, and especially the most marginalized.

Bibliography

Appleby, G.A., and J.W. Anastas. 1998. *Not Just a Passing Phase.* New York: Columbia University Press.

Bagley, C., and P. Tremblay. 1997. "Victim to Abuser: Mental Health and Behavioral Sequels of Child Sexual Abuse in a Community Survey of Young Adults Males." *Child Abuse and Neglect* 18, no. 8: 683–97.

– 1997a. "Suicidal Behaviors in Homosexual and Bisexual Males." *Crisis* 18, no. 1: 24–34.

Becker, Howard S. 1963. *Outsiders.* Glencoe, Ill.: Free Press.

Bell, Alan, and Martin Weinberg. 1978. *Homosexualities: A Study of Diversity among Men and Women.* New York: Simon & Schuster.

Boswell, J. 1994. *Same-Sex Unions in Premodern Europe.* New York: Vintage Books.

– 1980. *Christianity, Social Tolerance and Homosexuality.* Chicago: University of Chicago Press.

Clermont, M. 1996. *Santé, bien-être et homosexualité.* Ministère de la santé et des services sociaux, no. 26, coll. Études et analyses.

Cochran, S., and V. Mays. 2000. "Lifetime Prevalence of Suicide Symptoms and Affective Disorders among Men Reporting Same-

Sex Sexual Partners: Results from NHANES III. *American Journal of Public Health* 90, no. 4: 573–8.

Cyrulnik, Boris. 1999. *Un merveilleux malheur.* Paris: Odile Jacob.

Dorais, Michel. 1999. *Éloge de la diversité sexuelle.* Montreal: VLB Éditeur.

– 2002. *Don't Tell: The Sexual Abuse of Boys.* Montreal and Kingston: McGill-Queen's University Press.

Dorais, M., and P. Berthiaume. 1998. "Le vécu homosexuel: Les résultats d'un sondage auprès de 125 lecteurs du magazine RG." *RG* (July).

Durkheim, Émile. [1897] 1952. *Suicide.* Reprint, London: Routledge and Kegan Paul.

Éribon, Didier. 1999. *Réflexions sur la question gay.* Paris: Éditions Fayard.

Flynn Saulnier, Christine. 1998. "Prevalence of Suicide Attempts and Suicidal Ideation among Lesbian and Gay Youth." *Violence and Social Injustice against Lesbian, Gay and Bisexual People*, ed. L.M. Sloan and N.S. Gustavsson. New York: Haworth Press.

Garofalo, R., R. Wolf, S. Kessel, J. Palfrey, and R. DuRant. 1998. "The Association between Health Risk Behaviors and Sexual Orientation among a School-Based Sample of Adolescents." *Pediatrics* 101, no. 5: 895–902.

Garofalo, R., R. Wolf, M. Lawrence, and S. Wissow. 1999. "Sexual Orientation and Risk of Suicide Attempts among a Representative Sample of Youth." *Archives of Pediatric and Adolescent Medicine* 153, no. 5: 487–93.

Goffman, Erving. 1965. *Stigma: Notes on the Management of Spoiled Identity.* Englewood Cliffs, New Jersey: Prentice Hall.

Gouvernement du Canada, Conseil permanent de la jeunesse. 1994. *Le suicide au Canada.* Groupe d'étude sur le suicide au Canada.

Gouvernement du Québec. 1995. *Le point sur la délinquance et le suicide chez les jeunes.*

Gouvernement du Québec, Direction générale de la Santé publique. 1997. *S'entraider pour la vie – Proposition d'une stratégie québécoise d'actions face au suicide.* Consultation document.

Gouvernement du Québec, Ministère de la Santé et des Services sociaux. 2000. *Résultats de l'enquête portant sur les personnes décédées par suicide au Québec entre le 1er septembre et le 31 décembre 1996.*

Harris, M.B. 1997. *School Experiences of Gay and Lesbian Youth.* New York: Harrington Park Press.

Harry, Joseph. 1994. "Parasuicide, Gender, and Gender Deviance." In *Death by Denial*, ed. G. Remafedi. Boston: Alyson Publications.

Hirigoyen, Marie-France. 2000. *Stalking the Soul: Emotional Abuse and the Erosion of Identity.* Translated by Helen Marx. New York: Helen Marx Books.

Hite, Sheree. 1983. *The Hite Report on Male Sexuality.* New York: Knopf.

Janus, S.S., and C.L. Janus. 1993. *The Janus Report on Sexual Behavior.* New York: John Wiley & Sons.

Jay, K., and A. Young. 1977. *The Gay Report: Lesbians and Gay Men Speak Out about Their Sexual Experiences and Lifestyles.* New York: Summit.

Kinsey, A., W. Pomeroy, and E. Martin. 1948. *Sexual Behavior in the Human Male.* Philadelphia: W.B. Saunders.

Laumann, E.O., and J.H. Gagnon, R.T. Michael, and S. Michaels. 1994. *The Social Organization of Sexuality: Sexual Practices in the United States.* Chicago: University of Chicago Press.

Leymann, Heinz. 1996. *Mobbing.* Paris: Éditions du Seuil.

Lipkin, Arthur. 1999. *Understanding Homosexuality, Changing Schools.* Boulder, Colo.: Westview Press.

Los Angeles Suicide Prevention Center. 1986. *Problems of Suicide among Lesbian and Gay Adolescents.*

Maalouf, Amin. 1998. *Les identités meurtrières.* Paris: Grasset.

Ministère de la Santé et des Services sociaux. 1997. *Orientations ministérielles: L'adaptation des services sociaux et de santé aux réalités homosexuelles.* Québec: Gouvernement du Québec.

Ministère de l'Éducation du Québec [MEQ]. 2000. *Programme des programmes pour les écoles primaires.*

Muehrer, Peter. 1995. "Suicide and Sexual Orientation: A Critical Summary of Recent Research and Directions for Future Research." *Suicide and Life-Threatening Behavior* 25 (Supplement): 72–81.

Otis, J., R. Noël, R. Lavoie, R. LeClerc, B. Turmel, M. Alary, and R. Remis. 2000. *Suicide and Social Vulnerability to HIV Infection among Gay and Bisexual Men in Montreal.* Working document. Montreal: N.p.

Plummer, David. 1999. *One of the Boys: Masculinity, Homophobia, and Modern Manhood.* New York: Haworth Press.

Remafedi, Gary, ed. 1994. *Death by Denial: Studies of Suicide in Gay and Lesbian Teenagers.* Boston: Alyson Publications.

Remafedi, G., J. Farrow, and R. Deisher. 1991. "Risk Factors for Attempted Suicide in Gay and Bisexual Youth." *Pediatrics* 87, no. 6: 869–75.

Remafedi, G., S. French, M. Story, M. Resnick, and R. Blum. 1998. "The Relationship between Suicide Risk and Sexual Orientation: Results of a Population-Based Study." *American Journal of Public Health* 88, no. 1: 57–60.

Savin-Williams, R.C. 1994. "Verbal and Physical Abuse As Stressors in the Lives of Lesbian, Gay Male, and Bisexual Youths: Associations with School Problems, Running Away, Substance Abuse, Prostitution, and Suicide." *Journal of Consulting and Clinical Psychology* 62, no. 2: 261–9.

Spencer, Colin. 1995. *Homosexuality: A History.* New York: Harcourt Brace.

Tremblay, Pierre. 1995. "The Homosexuality Factor in the Youth Suicide Problem." Paper presented to the Sixth Annual Conference of the Canadian Association for Suicide Prevention, Banff, October, 1995. Internet: http://www.qrd.org/qrd/www/youth/tremblay/ and http://www.sws.soton.ac.uk/gay-youth-suicide/tremblay.htm.

Tremblay, Pierre, with R. Ramsay. 2000. "The Social Construction of Male Homosexuality, Related Suicide Problems and Research

Proposals for the Twentieth Century." Eleventh Annual Sociological Symposium on Deconstructing Youth Suicide, San Diego State University, March 2000.

Vincke, J., and K. Van Heeringen. 1998. "Suicidal Ideation and Behavior among Homosexual Adolescents and Young Adults: A Comparative Study." Paper presented at the Seventh European Symposium on Suicide and Suicidal Behavior.

Welzer-Lang, Daniel. 1994. *L'homophobie: La face cachée du masculin.* In *La peur de l'autre en soi: Du sexisme à l'homophobie.* by D. Welzer-Lang, P. Dutey, and M. Dorais. Montreal: VLB Éditeur.

Index

abandonment, fear of, 50

abuse, 25, 36, 37, 43, 53, 63, 71, 81, 83, 91, 107; of alcohol, 28, 29, 45, 46, 54, 55, 68; of drugs, 28, 29, 31, 32, 45–7, 55, 56, 67, 68; physical, 6, 7, 24, 41, 43, 47, 58–60, 62, 81; psychological, 41, 58–60, 62, 85; sexual, 30, 55, 56, 81, 82; verbal, 34, 35

academic success, 87

acceptance, 46, 57, 58

adaptive scenarios, 37–49

addiction, 28, 29, 48

adoption rights, 107, 108

aggression, 42

AIDS, 30, 45, 69, 98, 108–10

Alexander, 70

Anastas, J.W., 95

anger, 46, 61

anonymity, 64

anxiety, 42, 62, 75, 80

Appleby, G.A., 95

asexual behaviour, 19, 38, 48, 77

assault, 43, 60–3, 65, 76, 81, 104

auto-oppression, 18

axes of suicide (Durkheim), 17

Bagley, C., 9, 10, 30, 56

Becker, Howard, 19–21, 77, 87, 88

Bell, A., 10, 11, 13

Berthiaume, P., 13

blame, 63, 69

Boswell, J., 87

bullying, 22, 32

"Chameleon," 37, 44–9, 51, 76, 77, 80

Christian, 37, 45, 46

Claude, 52, 53

climate of understanding, 58

Cochran, S., 11

coming out, 13, 21, 24, 36, 46, 65, 100, 113; fear of, 51

conformity, 44

conversion to heterosexuality, attempted, 42

counselling, 100, 101

courage, 62, 80, 88

Cyrulnik, Boris, 75, 83, 93

Denis, 46, 56–8

depression, 31, 32, 39, 40, 42, 45, 47, 52, 62, 75, 81

deprivation, 6, 50, 52, 58, 74, 75, 78, 79

desire: sexual, 40, 41; to be "authentic," 44–6

determination, 85

deviance, 19–22, 25, 80

discredited homosexual attributes, 18, 75

discrimination, 19, 82, 84, 87; countering of, 88; elimination of, 111; protection from, 108

discussion groups, 65, 88

disguised homosexual attributes, 18, 19

disruptive behaviour, 61

diversity, sexual, 92–4, 97–9, 103, 104, 109, 113, 114

Dominic, 66, 67

Dorais, Michel, 13, 30, 81, 85, 103

double life, 65

drug overdose, 39,

Durkheim, Émile, 15–18, 89

early-identified, homosexual orientation, 33–7, 41, 51, 53, 58, 71, 99

educational programs: for educational institutions 109; for police, 99, 101, 109; for schools, 92–7; for teachers and other professionals, 97–9, 103, 109–11; for youth, 102, 103

effeminophobia, 25, 34, 98, 104; ending of, 97

equality, 6, 94, 96, 114

Éribon, Didier, 70

Eric, 65, 66

exhaustion, 74, 81

exclusion, 16, 17, 19, 77

expulsion, 51

"fag," 3, 19, 33, 35, 37, 40–3, 47, 57, 59–61, 63, 67, 70, 72, 73, 79, 84

fear, 24, 42; dealing with, 100; living in, 58, 101; of abandonment, 50; of being identified, 47, 71, 82, 96; of blame, 76; of deceiving, 39; of embarrassment, 38; of harassment, 40; of humiliation, 71; of parents, 53, 54; of stigmatization, 74, 78

Flynn Saulnier, Christine, 23, 24
forgiveness, 39, 55

Gaétan, 64, 65
Gai Écoute/Gay Line, 102, 111–13
Garofalo, R., 11
gay bars, 36, 64
gay community, 25, 65, 66
gay organizations, 86
gay teachers, 3, 61
Gay Village, Montreal, 64, 66, 88
gay youth group, 88
gender; conformable, 36; issues, 93, 96, 99; nonconformity, 35, 37, 62; role expectations, 25; stereotypes, 33, 34
Goffman, Erving, 18, 19, 37, 38, 41, 77, 80
Gouvernement du Québec, 108; Conseil permanent de la jeunesse, 9; Direction générale de la santé publique, 9; Ministère de la Santé et des Services sociaux, 98, 109, 110
grief, 5, 82
GRIS (Groupe de recherches et d'information sociale, Chaudière-Appalache), 91
Guillaume, 55, 56
guilt, 5, 47

harassment, 58, 60, 62, 71, 77, 81, 106; effects of, 22, 84;

moral, 22, 23, 31, 32, 41, 42, 75; protection from, 95; risk of, 23, 40
Harris, M.B., 62
Harry, Joseph, 10
hatred, 6, 42, 69, 96, 97, 104; of self, 80, 95, 104, 105
heterosexual, 19; expectations, 38; norm, 20, 23; status, 77
hidden life, 64, 65
Hilaire, 41, 42, 53, 60, 61
Hirigoyen, Marie-France, 22
Hite, Shere, 11, 91
HIV. See AIDS
homelessness, 74, 81
homophobia, 60; challenging of, 106–14; comments, 3, 50; as a disguise, 47; ending, 97; environment, 13, 48, 52, 60, 63, 91, 98, 104, 107; and hatred, 95; linked to suicide, 5, 6, 9, 12, 13, 23, 24, 26, 31; rejecting, 47–9, 86; and psychopathologies, 24; as a social reaction, 24
homosexual: accused of being, 21, 70; attributes of, 16–18, 25, 34, 35, 38, 84, 86; desires, 40; fear of revealing, 51; hidden relationships, 47; identified by others as, 8, 20, 23, 33, 37, 41, 90; link with suicide, 5, 6, 9, 12, 13, 23, 24, 26, 31, 102, 106; non-acceptance, 65; parents,

57; public image of, 68, 71, 73;
refusal to accept, 42, 45, 48; revealed as, 39, 40, 44; self-acceptance, 47–9, 65, 72, 84;
self-identify as, 8, 36, 90, 91;
sensitization, 62; statistics, 91;
stigmatization, 5, 25, 34, 68
hope, 88
hopelessness, 74, 81
hostile environment, 80, 84
humiliation, 3, 43, 71
humour, 85

identity construction, 21, 75, 88
impostor, 44, 47
inclusive language, 93, 94
indifference, 75, 76, 99
injustice, 47, 84, 87
insults, 63, 71, 72, 81
internalization, 86, 87; of expectations, 18
Internet sites, 4, 12
intervention, 20, 58, 63, 81, 95;
professional, 24. *See also* non-
intervention
intimidation, 101
intolerance, 7, 33, 82, 95, 99;
confronting, 89, 103, 104, 107
invisibility, 80
isolation, 6, 22, 25, 54, 56, 59, 63,
67, 74–83; overcoming, 88–90

Janus Report, 11, 92

Jay, K., 13
Jean-Francois, 38, 39, 82
Jean-Michel, 47, 48, 63
Jean-Phillippe, 3–5
Jean-Paul, 85–6
Johnny, 85

Kinsey study, 11, 20, 24, 25, 92

labelling, 37, 41
Lambda Youth, 65, 88, 102
later-identified homosexual orientation, 33, 36–8, 44, 53, 58,
71
Laumann, E.O., 11, 92
laws, 6, 20, 94; challenging of
discriminatory, 107, 113
Leymann, Heinz, 22
life situations, 50–73; family,
50–8; schools, 50, 58–63; social environment, 50, 63–7;
social representations of homosexuality, 50, 68–73
loneliness, 77, 78
Louis, 35, 60
lying to self, 44

Maalouf, Amin, 94
Marc, 34, 54, 59
Mario, 84
Martin, 36
masculinity, 23, 25, 39, 40, 43,
60, 70, 77, 79, 95, 97, 99

mask-wearing, 44, 47, 48

Mays, V., 11

media, 6, 68, 72, 73, 79, 80, 104–6, 111, 112

mental dysfunction, 81

Ministère de l'Éducation du Québec, 92

Ministère de la Santé et des Services sociaux, 98, 109, 110

mobbing, 22, 23

negative self-image, 54

Nicholas, 3, 5, 82

non-intervention, 40, 41, 60, 62, 75, 76, 81, 91, 107

norms, 20, 23, 24; transgression of, 77

Omega Cohort, 12, 13, 56

oppression, 21, 69

ostracism, 3, 6, 23, 24, 35, 43, 47, 51, 57, 68, 76–8, 83–5, 101; confronting, 89

Otis, J., 12, 13

outsiders, 19, 20, 59

overdosing, 39, 43, 61

paedophile, 70

Patrice, 40

"Perfect Boy," 37–41, 48, 49, 51, 76, 77, 80

perfectionist, 48

personality conflict, 22

physical abuse, 24, 41, 43, 47, 59, 60, 62, 81

physical harm, 6, 22, 41, 59

Pinard, Daniel, 112

Plummer, David, 23, 91

police, 20, 95, 99, 101, 109

pornography, 70

powerlessness, 41

prejudice, 22, 23, 68, 72, 75, 91, 95, 100, 104

professional intervention, 24

prostitution, 55, 100

protective factors, 83, 90

psychological abuse, 41, 59, 60, 62, 85

psychological dysfunction, 81

public inquiry, 108

public revelation of sexual orientation, 21, 106

Quebec Charter of Rights and Liberties, 100, 108

rape, 55

"Rebel," 37, 47–9, 76, 80, 85, 86

rejection, 37, 40, 67, 77; fear of, 36, 38, 51, 75; by children, 34, 43, 58, 59, 78; by father, 53, 54, 56, 81; by families, 24, 32, 38, 39, 50–5, 57, 58, 65, 68, 70, 76, 78; by mother, 54, 55; from religion, 69, 70, 104; from social environment, 18, 31, 64; from workplace, 66; of self, 46; of sexuality, 42, 48

relationships, importance of, 85

religious convictions, 52, 69

Remafedi, Gary, 9, 11, 13

resiliency factors, 83–90, 93

ridicule, 41, 60, 62, 81

rights, 22, 82, 85, 94, 95, 100, 104, 108

role models, 61, 62, 73, 92, 102, 104, 112; lack of, 68, 72, 79, 80, 92, 102, 104

Safe Places, 102

safe environment, 96

same-sex unions, 107

scapegoat, 35, 43, 77, 81

school dropout, 86, 91, 96, 100

selection criteria, 27

self-esteem, 58, 86; problems with, 49

self-hatred, 46, 80

self-image, 54

self-perception, 18, 21, 25, 31, 33, 34, 86

sensitization: campaigns, 6, 81, 103; programs, 98, 101, 103, 109–13

Serge, 34, 35, 43

sexism, 63, 97, 98, 104

sexual abuse, 30, 55, 56, 81, 82

sexual activity, 91

sexual desires, 24, 38, 41, 91, 104; hiding of, 45, 80

sexual orientation, 36, 44, 46, 91

sexual violence, 55

shame, 5, 53, 57, 61, 74–83, 89, 90, 92

shelters, 101

silence, 76, 81, 82, 99

situational conflicts, 22

social dimension attributes, 17, 17

social expectations, 77

social integration, 16–18, 93; problems with, 46, 51

social rules and regulation, 16–18

solidarity, 88

Spencer, Colin, 87

statistics, 9–13

Stephane, 42, 69, 70

stereotype, 33, 34, 68, 72

Steve, 54, 55

stigma, 18, 19, 36, 41, 68, 77, 83

stigmatization, 97; attributes, 18, 38; by contagion, 41; countering, 90; double, 105; fear of, 5; homosexual, 5, 23, 25, 36, 74–82; response to, 19; social, 79

study sample, 8, 9, 27–31

substance abuse, 28, 29, 31, 32, 45–7, 54–6, 67, 68

suffering, 18, 39, 58, 63, 82

suicide; as a solution, 47, 76; attempted, 5, 8, 23, 24, 28, 39,

40, 42–4, 48, 50, 52, 55–7, 60,
61, 64, 67, 71, 74, 75, 80–2,
104, 107; completed, 3–6, 30,
107; contemplated, 23, 42, 45,
51, 100; definition of, 15, 16;
factors leading to, 83; four
types of, 16, 17; ideation, 47,
50, 53, 54, 56, 62, 67–9; link
with homosexuality or ho-
mophobia, 5, 6, 9, 12, 13, 23,
24, 26, 31; methods of, 30; motivation, 31, 82; preventing, 15,
90–114; risk factors, 90; social
phenomenom, 15, 16; statistics, 9–13
suicidologists, 106
support: from groups, 6, 65, 85,
86, 88, 100, 111–13; lack of, 50,
51, 53, 58, 68; systems, 23, 24,
89
supportive parents, 4, 45–9, 56–
58
survival strategies, 37–49
Sylvain, 35, 59, 60, 62

teachers: intervention by, 61, 62;
openly gay, 92, 102; non-intervention by, 3, 60, 62, 75, 76,
91, 107; sympathy, 3, 5, 35, 61,
62

therapy, psychological, 28
"Token Fag," 37, 41–3, 48, 49,
60, 76–8
tolerance, 80
transgression, sexual, 20, 21
traumatic experiences, 35, 69, 75,
85
Tremblay, Pierre, 9, 10, 12, 24,
30, 56

triggering event, 82

unsafe sex, 55, 66

victimization, 75, 107, 114
violence, 31, 41–3, 53, 54, 58, 60,
62, 63, 66, 75, 79, 81, 85, 95,
100–2, 104, 107
vulnerability, 52, 70

Weinberg, M., 10, 11, 13
working group, 111
workplace, 63

Young, A., 13
youth group, 102
youth services, 101–3